Perfect "10"

Perfect "10"

The Ten Commandments for Graduates

Brent D. Earles

BAKER BOOK HOUSE
Grand Rapids, Michigan 49506

This is for the one person who shares my memories of growing up, and who sympathized with my struggle to keep the Fifth Commandment.

Dana,
when it comes to sisters, you're a "Perfect 10"

Contents

Preface

Commandments?" you may be moaning—"I don't want to read a book about commandments." I think I know where you're coming from. The whole idea of a command sounds bossy and negative. Right? And at this stage in your life, you have grown a bit tired of always being told what to do. That's a natural and acceptable attitude.

Here's what I've decided to do. The book is made up of ten sections—one for each commandment. Each section has three chapters, designed to give you a practical slant on the individual commands God first gave to Moses. As you read, you will easily find meaningful ways to apply those Old Testament laws to your New Testament life in Christ.

It is wrong to think that Jesus trashed the Ten Commandments. In fact, nine of them are repeated in the New Testament (all but the Sabbath commandment, which had a very specific purpose for Israel; it was to be a sign of their deliverance from Egypt [Exod. 31:16–17; cf. Deut. 5:15]). Jesus himself gladly obeyed the commandments. Furthermore, he had some salty words for anybody who thought he was trying to tear down the Law of Moses:

"Do not think that I have come to abolish the Law or the Prophets; I have not come to abolish them but to fulfill them. I tell

9

you the truth, until heaven and earth disappear, not the smallest letter, not the least stroke of a pen, will by any means disappear from the Law until everything is accomplished. Anyone who breaks one of the least of these commandments and teaches others to do the same will be called least in the kingdom of heaven, but whoever practices and teaches these commands will be called great in the kingdom of heaven" (Matt. 5:17–19).

Did you catch all that? He came to fulfill the Law, and we are supposed to live it and teach it. These commandments are not so much *rules* as they are *a way of life*. They are moral principles that point out the path of true righteousness. You see, before Jesus came, the best that people could muster up was outward rituals and traditions. Some of them had great faith but failed miserably at obeying the Law. By the time Jesus was born, spiritual ceremonies had become pretty boring. A real joke.

What happened? Well, Jesus began an exciting ministry unlike anything seen in Israelite history. It rocked all the boats of tradition. In reality, Jesus was not a radical. He simply loved and lived the Law from the heart. They had the commandments on the outside; Jesus had them from the inside out.

Christ was bringing the Law to life. As he lived, he was fulfilling God's "rules." As he died and arose, he made the fulfillment complete. We are to become everything that he was and is. As we do, we fulfill the commandments from the heart. Just as Jesus did!

Only in our Savior can we have true righteousness. Certainly not from merely keeping a bunch of ceremonies! However, that doesn't mean we can skip over the Ten Commandments. The "smallest letter" and the "least stroke of a pen" are still there for us. But how does it all apply to us today?

The Law was God's Old Covenant. In other words, it was his agreement with people who lived before Christ came. Jesus' death brought the blossoming of a broader, freer agreement. This is called the New Covenant, and it is written in Jesus' blood. Some people like to say that this new agreement means we don't have to pay attention to the laws of the old one anymore. But they're wrong! The Old Covenant was a bud; the New Covenant brought it to flower.

Question: What's the difference between then and now? Under the old plan God wrote his commandments on hard stone tablets. Today, when a person comes to Christ, the tablets are broken and God writes his laws upon the heart. Therefore, no Christian should despise God's laws. Heavy stuff, huh?

Why write a book about the Ten Commandments for graduates? That's a fair question. I'm interested in giving essential stuff to graduates. Some of it will be poetic; some will be philosophical; some will reel off one platitude after another; and some will routinely fall in line with the words of other congratulaters. But I want to give you something very unusual. Something relevant. Something special. Something you can use now and twenty years from now.

So this is a look at a beefy subject in a way you will enjoy seeing it. This book presents a lifestyle—not one with a ball and chain, but one that frees you to taste life fully. This is an invitation—not one that asks you to be conformed to a drab existence, but one that urges you to be transformed into a deeply satisfied person.

You need one thing to really get the most out of what you are about to read: a big appetite. Are you hungry for life and the joy of living it? Then grab a spiritual fork and dig in!

Introduction

The Chapter Before Chapter One

And God spoke all these words: "I am the LORD your God, who brought you out of Egypt, out of the land of slavery" (Exod. 20:1–2).

Don't skip over this chapter! Even though you may not read the other chapters in any particular order, this one is set apart for a special reason. Everything that follows revolves around this chunk of the book. Understand this and you will get the rest; omit this and you will miss the whole message.

Before God dictated the Ten Commandments, he reminded the Israelites how they got out of Egypt—by his grace! Moses didn't waltz into Egypt with an escape-from-Alcatraz blueprint. The people dug no underground tunnels from Egypt to the Red Sea. Aaron had no crack commando team to lead through the bullrushes while Moses gave air cover with an attack-force Airwolf. And Pharaoh didn't one day up and decide to become Humanitarian of the Year by letting the people go. The Israelites' freedom was God's work alone.

Of course, God did have a few war games of his own. The price the Egyptians paid for trying to hold Israel hostage was a dear one. The ten plagues turned their land into a frog-fly-and-locust paradise. Huge hail balls bombarded the country, while slime oozed grossly from the boils of the stricken people. When all the firstborn died, except those protected by the blood of an innocent lamb, the war was nearly over and Pharaoh was glad to let the people go.

A few days later he had a change of mind. He assembled a

powerful army and took off after the Israelites. When he caught up with them, he pinned their backs against a wall. In this case, the wall was the Red Sea. They were scared to death, to put it mildly. But over the maniacal laughter of Pharaoh and his men, they could hear Moses saying:

... "Do not be afraid. Stand firm and you will see the deliverance the LORD will bring you today. The Egyptians you see today you will never see again. The LORD will fight for you; you need only to be still" (Exod. 14:13–14).

That last sentence is the exclamation point of God's grace: "The Lord will fight for you; *you need only to be still*." Plainly, the people didn't have to do a thing to be saved but stand still. And exactly what did the Lord do to rescue them? A little-bittie miracle—he parted the Red Sea! When the Egyptian army came chasing them across the dry ground, God rolled the waters over them in one mighty surge. In moments the battle screams were silenced and the massive body of water became placid with a reflection of blue sky. The Israelites were free as birds.

Our "Egypt" is the worldly system that surrounds us. Our "Pharaoh" is none other than Satan himself. And our chains of bondage are the fetters of sin. *Question:* How on earth can we get free from such a straitjacket existence?

First of all, spiritual freedom does not begin on earth. Believing that one can be saved from a tormented eternity simply by keeping the Ten Commandments is a big mistake. God never meant to give people the impression that salvation can come through being a goodie-goodie. That's why he reminded the Israelites of his *grace* before giving them the *Law*. Grace comes down from heaven. It cannot be earned.

Then what purpose do the ten commandments serve? For one, they reveal the basic principles of living a decent life. I mean anyone with good sense knows that murder and stealing and adultery are the skull and crossbones in the medicine cabinet of life. If you swallow their poison, you swallow a bundle of heartaches.

God's commandments also provide an excellent map to lead us

to freedom. As we strain to keep God's tough standards, we realize how weak we are in this world of bondage. The compass arrow of the Law is pointing to Christ! Faith in him is the key to the lock on the chains that bind us.

> Before this faith came, we were held prisoners by the law, locked up until faith should be revealed. So the law was put in charge to lead us to Christ that we might be justified by faith. Now that faith has come, we are no longer under the supervision of the law (Gal. 3:23–25).

Although the Ten Commandments are only a small part of the Law of God, they are popular today. After all, they make such nice wall plaques. And that's about all some people get out of them: a pretty decoration.

Listen, before you attempt to build your life upon the principles of these commandments, be sure you have a good foundation. Pour your concrete in Christ. Then you can decorate your life with the moral beauty found in the principles of the Ten Commandments.

Just remember that to be saved you have only to stand still. Jesus finished the fight when he died on the cross and arose from the dead. Trust him and you're ready to begin. Otherwise, you're going to find God's commandments to be a Red Sea that never parts.

Not even a crack commando team would be able to save you.

PART **1**

The Devotion Commandment

"You shall have no other gods before me"
(Exod. 20:3).

1 Loyalty

Keepin' the Faith

Now it is required that those given a trust must prove faithful (1 Cor. 4:2).

St. Lucian was an odd bird, or so the story goes. It is said he was asked by his persecutors, "Of what country art thou?"

He answered, "I am a Christian."

"What is your occupation?"

"I am a Christian."

"Of what family?"

"I am a Christian."

Lucian may have been odd, but at least he was loyal. He was true till the end. Nothing or no one could make him stagger from his path in Christ.

That's what the first commandment is all about. Are you faithful to your Lord? Do you treasure your relationship with Christ above all other relationships? That's a tough one, isn't it? Because you're at the age when everything moves and changes fast. Tons of things are important to you, and it's hard to say from day to day which one ranks highest.

Today you may be thinking about college and the future. Tomorrow you might have your girlfriend or boyfriend on your mind. The next day you might wonder about the car you want to buy. The day after that your job gets prime attention. Before you realize what is happening, Jesus is taking a back seat in your life.

But disloyalty to our faith goes deeper than just having an over-crowded lifestyle. Such disloyalty occurs when something so distracts us that we give allegiance to it at the expense of knowing God. Whether on purpose or not, we trade the riches of our faith for a bowl of artificial and momentary happiness.

Esau did that. You know, Jacob's brother. He came home from a big safari hunt in the open country one day and found Jacob brewing some stew (Gen. 25:29–34). Esau was so hungry that he was willing to trade anything for a hot meal. He thought like many Americans do—with his belly.

So what did he trade? His birthright. That may not register big to you because our culture doesn't operate quite like theirs did. But, being the elder son, Esau was trading off all the privileges of his inheritance just for a short-lived dose of pleasure. Of course, it was Jacob, not Esau, whose family line became Israel. And it was Israel, the nation that began with one man and twelve sons, that received the Ten Commandments.

The moral of the story is that you'd better check out what's really important before cutting any hasty deals. When he pigged-out on Jacob's famous recipe, Esau was making a decision that would affect him the rest of his life. The world has a similar kettle cooking for you. If you let your appetite get strong enough for the things of earth, you will be tempted to cash in the fullness of Christ for a morsel of temporary happiness. And, if a good time gets to be a priority item for you—more popular than loyalty to the Lord—then be sure there's a "bowl of stew" awaiting you.

As you trek on, don't forget your inheritance. In Jesus Christ you have a wealth of eternal blessings being stored up for you. With Jesus as your Savior and Lord, you have the promise of sharing "in the inheritance of the saints in the kingdom of light" (Col. 1:12).

On top of that, by being a loyal servant of the Lord, you can add to your future inheritance. Check out Colossians 3:23–25 to see what I mean:

Whatever you do, work at it with all your heart, as working for the Lord, not for men, since you know that you will receive an inheritance from the Lord as a reward. It is the Lord Christ you are serving. Anyone who does wrong will be repaid for his wrong, and there is no favoritism.

It is a general principle of Scripture that a faithful person can earn rewards and add to his or her already-awesome inheritance. But it should also be noted that God does not play favorites: the loyal will receive extra rewards; the disloyal will receive nothing. The whole system is based upon keeping the faith.

One of the truest followers of Christ was the apostle Paul. He stayed loyal through the most awful circumstances. At the end of his life he sat in a lonely dungeon, waiting to be beheaded, and wrote these words:

> For I am already being poured out like a drink offering, and the time has come for my departure. I have fought the good fight, I have finished the race, I have kept the faith. Now there is in store for me the crown of righteousness, which the Lord, the righteous Judge, will award me on that day—and not only to me, but also to all who have longed for his appearing (2 Tim. 4:6–8).

Notice what he said: "I have kept the faith." That means he didn't sell out. At his lowest moments he would not swap the splendor of being a Christian for a second's worth of this world's beef stew. Paul had been given a trust—a personal relationship with a personal God—and he was faithful enough to share it with others. He guarded his trust, and it redoubled into a magnificent inheritance.

Recently I came across some sad words in the Psalms. It was a down time in Israel's history, and the songwriters were feeling gloomy. So they wrote this song: "Help, LORD, for the godly are no more; the faithful have vanished from among men" (Ps. 12:1). I stopped and prayed that such words would never be said of my generation. Nor of yours.

Even if it means being an odd bird.

2 Commitment

Custody of the Heart

Therefore, I urge you, brothers, in view of God's mercy, to offer your bodies as living sacrifices, holy and pleasing to God—which is your spiritual worship (Rom. 12:1).

. W. Tozer is remembered as one of the great Christians of the twentieth century. Among other writings is his famous *The Pursuit of God*. I have read it several times and still find that it makes my socks roll up and down. Try this stuff for example:

> Our woes began when God was forced out of his central shrine and "things" were allowed to enter. Within the human heart "things" have taken over. Men have now by nature no peace within their hearts, for God is crowned there no longer, but there in the moral dusk stubborn and aggressive usurpers fight among themselves for first place on the throne.*

That stings because it's right on target. Sometimes—after surrendering to the Lord, our God—we soon reclaim little pieces of our hearts and secretly hide them. We think God doesn't notice, but we're wrong.

*Used with permission of Christian Publications, Camp Hill, Pennsylvania

One of the purposes behind the first commandment was to teach dedication to the Lord. Dedication is a cousin to loyalty; it means having deep devotion to a single object, goal, or person. The committed Christian is completely given to Jesus Christ. He or she avoids things that threaten to mess up this relationship with the Lord.

Such dedication is unfashionable with a lot of graduates. To some, Jesus has become a mere garment. Like anything stylish, he is worn only for effect. When he is convenient to an occasion, he is taken out of the closet. Otherwise he just stays stuck on a hanger.

Childhood decisions to follow Christ are too often chucked out the window in the high school and college years. The pressures on people your age—not to mention plain old human curiosity—can cause the unraveling of a usually devoted Christian. Beer parties, pot, chances for sex and reckless freedom, all seem so inviting. Only those with heavy metal can resist and say a big loud "No!"

The shame and embarrassment brought on by the smart-aleck ridicule of ungodly peers can be hard to cope with. Their barbed arrows will eventually penetrate the cracks in your armor. Even the best-prepared Christians are wounded. The weak ones become victims. The unprepared become captives. The insincere become casualties.

Sure, living for Jesus is going to make you the butt of some cruel jokes. But let the fools rattle on. In time they will be stung by their own poison. Their missiles usually circle back, and verbal attacks upon a committed Christian have a strange way of becoming nasty boomerangs.

Unfortunately, there's a herd of believers who are satisfied with just a smidgen of religion. A dab of spirituality makes them feel comfortable with themselves. They slather it on like suntan lotion. Because they get cranky when constricted, they have trained their Christianity to conform to their personal lifestyle.

I think we can conclude that these people have missed the point of the first commandment. Not that I favor a rigid black-and-white outlook on life. I'm not suggesting a restrictive law that *forces* people to surrender to Christ. God is not a heavenly highway patrol-man, walking the spiritual beat with a nightstick made of lightning rods. If police action were used to keep Christians on the straight and narrow, then the whole spirit of the Devotion Commandment would be lost.

Give another glance at the verse heading this chapter.

The key phrase is: "In view of God's mercy." The verse did *not* say, "Offer your life to Christ, or else God will bust your head." In essence it says, "It only makes sense that we dedicate ourselves to God, when you think about how good he has been to us." God wants each of us to mold our lifestyles around *him* as the center.

That won't make us into clones of one another. You will keep your own unique individuality. Yet we all share a common commitment. With a common hope. With a common help. And with a common harmony. In Christ we share many alikenesses, but we remain very different. God would not have it any other way!

This common bond inspires us to cheer each other on. We grow to love those who love God as we do. All this is part of the mortar that keeps us from coming unglued in a sticky world. Without the encouragement of others as committed as we are, the demons "nuke" us until we feel like giving up. That's when our real commitment is about to be tested.

It can be a lonely road. A long road. But the genuinely devoted ones do not turn back. Or take side roads. Or regret being dedicated. Or mope around. Or pretend with phony faces. Something special motivates them. In the Christian's soul throbs an unquenchable thirst to know God and to love him even more! That throb turns commitment from a chore into a pleasure. The job becomes a joy.

One cannot be committed and hate that commitment at the same time. Total devotion is more a response to a wholehearted love for God than it is a graduation-book formula for trying your best. Commitment is a fruit, not a fertilizer.

What you have to ask yourself is: "Who has custody of my heart?"

3 Intimacy

Within the Veil

Even to this day when Moses is read, a veil covers their hearts. But whenever anyone turns to the Lord, the veil is taken away (2 Cor. 3:15–16).

I will never forget my wedding day. The bridesmaids came down the aisle one by one, followed by the ringbearer and flower girl. Those cute tots nearly stole the show, a beautiful reminder of how an innocent child will someday stand on the threshold of life's sacred vow of marriage. They represent the bride and groom as children in the memory of those who watched them grow up.

Anyway, back to my wedding ceremony. When the bridal march struck up and all the people stood, Jane stepped around the corner at the back entrance of the long church aisle. Silently my tears formed. Although I had known her for several years, I had never seen her so breathtakingly lovely.

In full-flowing white gown, she came slowly toward me. Everyone watched and smiled, but I couldn't see her face clearly. The delicate veil she wore allowed me to see only a bit more than a shadowed image of her face. My eyes searched through the fabric to meet hers as we exchanged tender smiles.

Talk about nervous! I could have used a beach towel to dry the palms of my hands. The ceremony seemed like a lifetime but took about twenty minutes. And then came the most intimate moment— the kiss. But first I had to lift that fragile veil!

What if it stuck to her face? What if it fell off her head? What if

23

it came apart? Why did she have to wear this confounded thing? How am I supposed to lift it up? Should I go gently, or should I just flop it back? These questions and ten thousand more darted back and forth across my brain during the fifteen seconds before I made my move.

Today I realize what the veil symbolized. It was a picture of everything that kept us from being one. The veil meant that we had families to leave. That we had new responsibilities to prepare for. That there were new things to learn about each other. That adjustments would have to be made. Sounds like a lot of trouble for one kiss, huh?

Once removed, we could see each other perfectly. It was a precious moment, because it meant we had just begun a life as intimate companions. The veil would never separate us again.

The Israelites had a terrible problem with the Ten Commandments. They couldn't see through them clearly. Behind the gauze of God's Law was God himself. Even the Jews who strictly obeyed the rules missed the message. The veil in the holy temple was an emblem of the veil that hung over their hearts. They were righteous. They watched every *p* and *q*. They dotted every Hebrew *i* and crossed every Hebrew *t* like good boys and girls, but they failed to get truly close to God.

These Jews liked ritual and ceremony too much. It was easy. It was comfortable. It was nice. It was better than being a heathen. The laws of Moses were neat stuff. But they became a veil for the Jews. Even to this day!

Jesus fixed that veil business for us. The moment he died, the veil in the holy temple ripped down the middle. Jesus was removing the blindfold. He was saying, "Now you can get to know God up close— intimately—through me!"

The shame of it all is that, like the Israelites, many of today's Christians like to keep Jesus at arm's length. Oh, they live pretty good lives. But a thin shroud hangs between them and the Lord.

Look through the haze of the first commandment. Go ahead. What do you see? I mean, what's this law all about? What is God trying to get across? Why did he say, "You shall have no other gods before me"?

Try this on for size: I think he was trying to get people to see how badly he wants to be important to us. And I don't mean second or third on our list. God was inviting people to begin an intimate friendship with him.

How well do you know Jesus? I'm not talking about facts and information you have memorized. How close are you to each other? Does he touch you? That is, does he reach your heart and soul? Does he heal your hurt emotions? Can you cry to him? Have you ever visualized him crying with you? Crying *for* you? Laughing with you? Laughing *at* you?

What is Jesus to you? Only your Savior? (I know that's a lot.) Merely your boss? How much of a veil separates you two? Have you gone beyond just saying "Howdy" to him when you pass him in the hallways of your prayer time? Is he more than an ornament of jewelry around your neck? More than a Sunday-morning church service? More than a "quickie" devotion?

When I lifted my wife's bridal veil, it signaled the beginning of a fantastic relationship. And when I stepped within the veil to really walk with Christ, it was the start of my most favorite friendship. All is not easy behind the veil. But I can see clearly now, and I fall down a lot less than some other folks. Get my drift?

By the way, for details about my wedding kiss, you'll have to ask my wife.

2

The God Commandment

"You shall not make for yourselves an idol in the form of anything in heaven above or on earth beneath or in the waters below. You shall not bow down to them or worship them; for I, the LORD your God, am a jealous God, punishing the children for the sin of the fathers to the third and fourth generation of those who hate me, but showing love to thousands who love me and keep my commandments" (Exod. 20:4–6).

Religion

The God-Concept

For you did not receive a spirit that makes you a slave again to fear, but you received the Spirit of sonship. And by him we cry, "Abba, Father" (Rom. 8:15).

In *King Henry V,* William Shakespeare penned these pesky lines:

> And what art thou, thou idol ceremony?
> What kind of god art thou, that suffer'st more
> Of mortal griefs than do thy worshippers?
> What are thy rents? what are thy comings-in?
> O ceremony! show me but thy worth.

Bingo! He nailed religion right on the head. Notice that I said "religion," not "Jesus Christ." These days there is a big difference between the two. Religion is a social playground, and Jesus Christ demands much more than a "We Are The World" God-concept. There's no sense in my pulling any punches, because he certainly didn't. Airheaded mush about the "brotherhood of man and our common Grandpa in the sky" is for nincompoops and dodo birds. If Jesus were here to listen to that flowery garbage, he would either laugh uproariously or break out in a righteous rash.

I bet I've raised your eyebrows. Good! Too many voices have remained silent about the church games that pass for godliness. Don't get me wrong—I believe in feeding the hungry and helping the poor. But those are things a person does as a result of having a vital relationship with the Lord, not simply out of an obligation to suffering humanity. People who are do-gooders do not necessarily have genuine connections with the Most High.

Virtually millions of people in this world have a totally warped understanding of God. Some think that God is so lovey-dovey that he won't hold any judgment-day ceremonies whatsoever. Others imagine him to be so terrifying that we must toe the mark or be tossed aside like dirty rags. Still others are caught up in glorious rituals and pretty religious garb.

World religion is a wild study, including some forms that involve so-called Christianity. Do you have any idea what kind of diverse practices various religious folks are counting on to fix them up with eternal bliss? Don't laugh—sincere worshipers take this jazz seriously.

Every year during a certain time, thousands pledge to quit doing something they enjoy. The self-denial is supposed to prove to God that they are trying to be religious.

Totem poles still exist in some uncivilized lands, and they are not just the teepee village statue. They are the worship center. Fireside dances are dedicated to cheer up these unhappy gods.

Have you ever been at a funeral where a fellow wearing ceremonial robes walked around swooshing incense smoke over the dead body?

Did you know that some towns in the world have a sort of prayer alarm? When the gong sounds, everybody drops down and starts praying.

Some religions require their worshipers to take time off for a pilgrimage. That is a trip to a designated holy land. It gives religious brownie points.

One belief, now centuries old, has followers paying money for prayers to shorten their stay in the dingy dungeon of afterlife called purgatory.

In some cases, "holy rollers" should be changed to *wholly* rollers. These types flop around uncontrollably and nearly foam at the mouth while jabbering baby-talk. All in the name of God.

Another doctrine tells couples they must get married in the central shrine to ensure God's ultimate blessings.

Space does not permit me to ramble on. I am sorry if I offended anyone, but somebody has to iron out the creases in our wrinkled concept of God. "Religion" and ceremonial practices are not what he is all about. It's your own business if you want to get wrapped up in rituals, but don't fool yourself into believing that God is so thrilled with them that he will overlook a weak-kneed faith or faulty lifestyle.

Trying to cram Old Testament culture into the twentieth century is off beam. What God requires has not changed, although he has never given hard-and-fast rules for how to go about it. God wants faith and fellowship and purity, not a bunch of play-acting. Authenticity is a matter of the heart.

Religion is not enough! It fails to even give us a focused picture of who God is. At best, it allows us to create God in our own image, so that he can't interfere with our lifestyles. Religion doesn't help us worship; it only makes us feel as if we're worshiping. Religion doesn't cleanse our sins; it only makes us think that we're clean. Religion doesn't really spotlight the walk with Christ; it only gives people a reason to say they are "Christians."

I know—don't tell me—I'm on my soapbox. But what most people call religion really bugs me because it's so plastic. Even kind, honest, decent, and moral people use it as a buy-off to keep from giving what God really wants. Themselves. No games, just humble adoration.

O ceremony! show me but thy worth.

5 Idolatry

Creatures Featured

Although they claimed to be wise, they became fools and exchanged the glory of the immortal God for images made to look like mortal man and birds and animals and reptiles (Rom. 1:22–23).

There is an old saying that goes something like this: "We shouldn't mistreat our idols; the gold comes off on our hands."

We are not without golden calves today. You heard me right! Do you remember the episode that was taking place in Israel's camp while Moses was up on Mount Sinai? On the mountaintop, God was carving the Ten Commandments in stone while Moses gazed on with amazement. Down below, the children of Israel were melting all their earrings and watches to make a golden calf. It was the ultimate creature-feature!

Believe this: when they got the shiny beast finished, they said, "These are your gods, O Israel, who brought you up out of Egypt" (Exod. 32:4). Then the next day they had a religious holiday. With huzzahs and hurrahs, they initiated their calf as a god. That is truly nuts! A person would have to be delirious to concoct such a thing, much less bow down to it.

When Moses came back from mountain climbing, the whole

mess gave him high blood pressure. He smashed the nice stone tablets on which God had written—right over the golden calf's head, perhaps. After that, he melted down the calf, ground the remains into powder, scattered it on the water, and made the people drink it. That put the idol right back where it started from—within each of them—for all idolatry begins with self.

Idol worship sounds like something heathen savages do in the remote jungles of another continent. Not always so. In fact, idolatry is very much alive and well in downtown U.S.A. Although it isn't as shockingly obvious as a golden calf, it exists nonetheless.

You see, the whole principle behind the second commandment is that God should not be replaced by anyone or anything. When you dump God and start shaping your life around another, that is idolatry. Want some examples? Okay, but you know I'll shoot straight from the hip. So be prepared.

Television is the plug-in god of masses. I don't mean occasional viewing; I'm talking about addiction! Hours of uninterrupted sponge-living are the benediction of the day for these "worshipers." Can't relate? Yesterday I was told of a man who carried his TV outside and then went back inside to set the house on fire. Guess we know who his "god" is. But he's not alone.

Rock music and its performers are the idols of countless thousands. Again, I'm talking about the ones who practically kneel at this "altar." Rock disciples spend hours glued daily to the radio and stereo or plugged in to a Walkman—doing nothing but listening, getting blasted, or buzzing off. Give them a video and they're in heaven.

We musn't forget the "green god," money. Some people live for the *almighty* dollar. Their whole life rises or falls on their bank account. All other things—including God—are ordered by their love of money. P.S.: One does not have to be wealthy to worship this graven image.

Ever hear of reincarnation? That's a form of idolatry: worshiping a life form. Come back as a cow, or octopus, or leafhopper, or pumpkin plant, or zebra, or crabgrass, and start working your way up. These idolators believe they will someday reincarnate as gods themselves. That pagan idea is as old as the hills.

One of the cults in this country believes in a family of gods. They believe God has a mama and daddy, brothers and sisters, aunts and uncles, and probably cousins. Evidently these gods have sex with each other. How sick! But if you really investigate the followers of Joe Smith, you'll find some pure, uncut idolatry.

Millions of people worship their church, bedecked with statues galore and patron saints by the dozens. This form of idol worship is the only thing they know. Without their strings of beads and religious relics, many of these people would be hopeless. But one must wonder about their "hope," despite their sincerity.

Nature worshipers. Ever meet one? The technical name for this type of idolatry is "pantheism." They revere the panorama—the scenic view. They don't really think God created the "Rocky Mountain high"; they think the "Rocky Mountain high" *is god*! "God is beauty; and beauty is God"—that is their motto. Sounds poetic, but something's wrong.

If Moses were here, he'd go crazy. Today's golden calves are not sitting out in plain sight, but people glorify them just the same. And folks don't take kindly to having their foolishness poured out for them. What looks good and feels good doesn't taste so great when it's scattered on the water to drink. In the eye it shines; in the mouth it grinds. Follow?

The God Commandment is not the Almighty's way of bending back our fingers until we kneel to him, but just his way of keeping the record straight. When it comes to being important, he wants to be first or nothing else. In fact, as far as he is concerned, he is either first or nothing at all.

God is not like us. He knows no in-between. People are either hot or cold toward him. Lukewarm becomes mouthwash. If you know what I mean.

The Book of Revelation contains one of the saddest verses in the

Bible. It is about the end of the world and how people will respond to God's judgment in that day. Listen to what it says:

> The rest of mankind that were not killed by these plagues still did not repent of the work of their hands; they did not stop worshiping demons, and idols of gold, silver, bronze, stone and wood—idols that cannot see or hear or walk (Rev. 9:20).

How awful that man will make idols to replace God to the very end, yet doesn't like to get the gold on his hands.

Lordship

"I AM," He Said

"I tell you the truth," Jesus answered, "before Abraham was born, I am!" (John 8:58).

I once heard the story of a young lady who stood talking to a guest speaker after his message on "Making Christ Your Lord." She was somewhat puzzled by his sermon and had to tell him her concern. "I'm afraid to give myself wholly to the Lord," she explained, "because he might do something like send me to China." Her slight laugh failed to hide her genuine fear.

The minister offered none of the usual pat answers, but rather a parable. He answered, "Suppose some frigid winter morning a little bird should come, half-frozen, pecking at your window, and should permit you to take it in and feed it, depending completely on you, what would you do? Would you grip it in your hand and crush it? Or would you nourish it to health and give it your love?"

With a smile, the young lady responded, "I think I get your point." She walked away with new insight.

Two years later she had the chance to meet the speaker again and couldn't wait to share all that God was doing in her life. Beaming, she said, "You probably don't remember me, but once I heard you speak on the lordship of Christ. Afterwards I told you I was afraid to give Christ my all, because he might send me to China."

"I remember you now," he nodded. "So what did you decide?"

"I decided to come in out of the cold and let the Lord have control of my life."

"Any complaints?" he asked.

"No. Never once have I regretted it." Then a wide grin lit her face, "And I am proud to say that I will be leaving for China next month."

Did that story merely confirm your suspicions that God really does send the obedient ones to a foreign country? I hope not, because there is a deeper message. When you truly submit to Christ, your life finds its richest rewards, regardless of how or where he leads. On the surface, doing God's will may not sound too thrilling, but underneath it all, joy swells. And it can only be known by those who experience it.

Of course, that Christ deserves to rule our lives cannot be denied. Take a gander at the New Testament verse that opens this chapter. Think for a moment about how that relates to the second commandment.

You have probably heard the ditty about the Old and New Testaments that goes: "The New is *concealed* in the Old, and the Old is *revealed* in the New." Well, here is a case in point.

Before Moses went to the peaks to receive the Ten Commandments—even before he led the people out of Egypt—he had a spectacular experience. Grab your Bible and turn to Exodus 3:1–15. Ready? Instantly you're sitting with Moses at the burning bush! (That's what I love about Scripture; it lets me join in!)

God has just instructed Moses to go to a foreign country. God's people are being held hostage in Egypt, and God wants Moses to set them free. As you might guess, Moses is a bit nervous about his mission. So he asks God, "What if everybody wants to know who sent me? What should I say?"

Then came God's famous answer: "God said to Moses 'I am who I am. This is what you are to say to the Israelites: "I AM has sent me to you" ' " (Exod. 3:14).

Did you catch that? God's name is "I AM." Now read John 8:58 again. Jesus said, ". . . before Abraham was born, *I am*!" (italics mine). Either Jesus needs to learn some grammar, or else he was trying to make a point. Which do you figure it was? His point: "Since

I am the '*I AM*,' I have the right to be your Lord." That makes sense.

But the question is: Is the Lord *your* Lord? You might be wondering just what that means. The lordship of Christ may be a new concept to you. Fair enough. Let's look it over:

Lordship does not entail slavery. We do become the Lord's servants, but not his mistreated slaves. Yielding to Christ does not mean that you lose your personality, dreams, and goals. It does not require that you become a faceless robot who marches around like a rigid zombie. Nor does it imply that you are destined to live a sad, poor, miserable life. But it does mean that you are willing to obey God's leading and—even more—that you *seek* it!

Lordship is not a call to "the ministry." Giving yourself wholly to Christ does not demand that you become a preacher or missionary or minister's spouse. God needs doctors, lawyers, teachers, factory workers, carpenters, marketing directors, managers, nurses, secretaries, writers, and soda jerks, too. He equally wants to be the Lord of everyone, regardless of what occupation he has gifted you for. Don't think that the white flag of surrender on your part means that God is necessarily calling you into the ministry. Although, if he is your Lord, you will be willing to do that. Won't you?

Lordship requires a certain lifestyle. If Jesus is Lord, then the natural thing to do is follow him. All choices and decisions are funneled first through his will. Self-centeredness is out the door. It's the "not my will but thine, Lord" adventure into living. The remarkable thing about this lifestyle is that Jesus knows exactly what can bring you the greatest fulfillment. As your loving Lord, he will lead you there. He has never yet taken a bird out of the cold and crushed it—and he never will.

To be sure, you will not bat .1000 on responding to Christ's Lordship. I'm not condoning stubbornness, just being realistic. Nobody's perfect. You will fail, and you will have to get up from your failure and brush yourself off. You will have to back up and start at square one. You will have to see it through the Lord's eyes. You will have to have faith.

You may even have to go to China.

3

The Praise Commandment

"You shall not misuse the name of the LORD your God, for the LORD will not hold anyone guiltless who misuses his name" *(Exod. 20:7).*

7 Attitude

Voice of the Heart

You were taught, with regard to your former way of life, to put off your old self, which is being corrupted by its deceitful desires; to be made new in the attitude of your minds (Eph. 4:22–23).

Someone has suggested that a new punctuation mark be introduced. It would be a strange combination of the question mark (?) and the exclamation point (!). This climactic symbol would be used after questions one can answer with only a shrug, a sneer, a sigh, or a stare of daggers. In other words, sarcastic questions requiring no verbal response. The proposed punctuation mark would be called an "interrobang," and would look something like this: ?

If the interrobang were to catch on, it would be the perfect grammatical highlight to questions like these:

Policeman to speeding motorist: "Where's the fire, buddy?"

Brother to sister who left the front door standing wide open: "Were you born in a barn?"

Guy to girl with a new hairdo: "I really like your hair. Did it get caught in a meat grinder?"

Senior citizen to hamburger-joint manager: "Where's the beef?"

Dentist to patient whose tooth he just drilled: "Did it hurt?"

Angry motorist to driver blocking his way: "Where did you get your license? Out of a box of Cracker Jacks?"

Patient upset with nurse's technique: "Do you think it is necessary to strike bone every time you give a shot, nurse?"

Pharisee trying to trap Jesus concerning taxes: "Is it right to pay taxes to Caesar or not?"

Sarcasm can be both funny and cruel. I suppose we have all used it, mostly in lighthearted situations. By the way, you can relax. This isn't going to be a chapter on the e-e-evils of sarcasm. Are you kidding? Wiping out sarcasm would mean the end of my writing career.

I've got something else in mind, something that relates to the third commandment. Something that comes across in our New Testament passage at the beginning of this chapter: a sarcastic outlook. Yeah, you read that right. These types see everything with an 'interrobang'.

Not pessimism, but a hard exterior in dealing with people. The Tough Guy or Mean Mama approach to things. It's what some people refer to as "carrying a chip on your shoulder." Confucius say, "Chip on shoulder come from block for head." Get it?

Let's call it by its cliché name: the bad attitude. After all, isn't that what provokes people to habitually abuse the Lord's name? When all else is said and done, it really boils down to an irreverent view of things. That's what it has to be. Otherwise, why would people so flippantly drag God's name through the mud? Because using God's name as a curse word is meant to show the ultimate contempt.

How about people who curse so much that they don't realize how bad it sounds? Perfect example. I figure that those who always revile, even when trying to be funny, must have a heart problem. Because attitude is the voice of the heart. What a person feels and thinks under it all will be broadcast loudly in his or her attitude.

The one who has served eviction papers on his (or her) "old self" will have a pleasant perspective. Oh, maybe he's bound to get miffed from time to time, but he recovers quickly. It doesn't blow him away. He doesn't become a smart-mouthed, cussing maniac, with drool dripping out of his attitude.

You may be wondering, "Exactly what is a bad attitude? Are there any handles that can help me get hold of its meaning?" Sure, I think so. How about Pharaoh, for example. Before the Ten Commandments, Moses had to do business with this guy. And you talk about a bad attitude! Pharaoh excelled at it! In fact, he was a perfect portrait of the old shoulder-chip theory:

> " 'Pharaoh's heart is unyielding' . . ." (Exod. 7:14). Characteristic: *Harsh stubbornness.*

> ". . . Pharaoh's heart became hard; he would not listen to Moses and Aaron. . . . Instead, he turned and went into his palace, and did not take even this to heart" (Exod. 7:22–23). Characteristic: *Know-it-all.*

> "But when Pharaoh saw that there was relief, he hardened his heart . . ." (Exod. 8:15). Characteristic: *"I couldn't care less."*

> "But this time also Pharaoh hardened his heart and would not let the people go" (Exod. 8:32). Characteristic: *"Nobody tells me what to do!"*

> "When Pharaoh saw that the rain and hail and thunder had stopped, he sinned again . . ." (Exod. 9:34). Characteristic: *"I'm not sorry for anything!"*

> ". . . but the LORD hardened Pharaoh's heart . . ." (Exod. 11:10). Characteristic: *"Don't preach to me!"*

Those are the marks of a person with an attitude problem. The hardest thing about this is getting such a person to admit it. Even those who know it's true will try to sluff it off. Press the point too far and they will explode. All bad attitudes have short fuses.

God is not just protecting his name with the third commandment; he is implying that we should be joyful. That we should praise him. That we should have a bright outlook on things. That we should not blow up all of life with an interrobang!

⑧ Talk

Dialogue on Dialogue

If anyone considers himself religious and yet does not keep a tight rein on his tongue, he deceives himself and his religion is worthless (James 1:26).

A famous painting of the late 1930s has Adolph Hitler giving a speech to throngs of his Nazi disciples. It's a bland theme at first look, but a lingering observation reveals the fervor of Hitler's oratory skill. One can see the creases in his face and almost feel the hate being poured before his hearers. The longer one looks, the louder the cries of rage peal forth from the artwork. Boldly the swastika—the twisted cross—begins to pound up out of the frozen scene. And the artist's caption takes on profound meaning: IN THE BEGINNING WAS THE WORD.

The Praise Commandment is a reminder that our words provide our best self-portrait. Or worst, depending on the character. By simply listening to a person talk, you can tell a lot about him or her.

Let me show you what I mean. Meet Nabal, a thug and ingrate. The Bible says he was "surly and mean in his dealings" (1 Sam. 25:3). Now isn't that an awful thing to have said about you? But it wasn't an exaggeration. Characterizing Nabal as "surly" would be like describing the Jolly Green Giant as "tall."

Anyway, if you'd like to dig up the story, it's found in 1 Samuel 25. Nabal was a rich sheep rancher. David was the king-to-be on the block, and he had instructed a group of his men to guard Nabal's shepherds—just a kind gesture to help the ol' boy out. When sheep-shearing time came, Nabal forgot David's kindness and sent the good soldiers on their not-so-merry way. He chewed them out and said he'd never heard of David. Nice guy, Nabal.

This didn't set well with the Goliath-killer. David told his men to lace up their sword holsters for a high-noon showdown. Four hundred took off for the Desert of Maon. I guess David wanted a good show of strength. Whatever the case, if he had it his way, the Desert of Maon would soon be called the Desert of Moan. Because Nabal would be *moaning* with regret.

As you might have concluded, these two were not exactly on good speaking terms. One had already said and done some things for which he was about to pay. The other was on his way to saying and doing some things that he, too, would probably regret. The story might be Old Testament, but it still happens every day.

The plot thickens: Nabal's shepherds unloaded the story on Nabal's wife, Abigail. (This is great stuff! And it isn't even fiction!). After telling her about Nabal's insulting behavior, they added, "Now think it over and see what you can do, because disaster is hanging over our master and his whole household. *He is such a wicked man that no one can talk to him*" (1 Sam. 25:17, italics mine).

They sure knew the truth about Nabal. His filthy mouth had gotten him into trouble more than once. Know the type?

Abigail knew it, too. She fetched two hundred loaves of bread, two skins of wine, five roasted lambs, five bushels of grain, a hundred raisin cakes, and two hundred Fig Newtons. Then she grabbed a blazing donkey to meet David. When she arrived, Abigail fell on her knees and called David her master, begging him to rethink his plan. Her speech was magnificent.

Here's part of it:

"May my lord pay no attention to that wicked man Nabal. He is just like his name—his name is Fool, and folly goes with him. . . . Please forgive your servant's offense. . . . When the LORD has done for my master [David] every good thing he promised concerning him and has appointed him leader over Israel, my master [David] will not have on his conscience the staggering burden of needless bloodshed or of having avenged himself . . ." (1 Sam. 25:25, 28, 30–31).

David was touched by her thoughtfulness. He thanked her for keeping him from doing a foolish act of violence. Her *words* changed David's heart. Words have that power. No wonder Scripture says "she was an intelligent and beautiful woman" (1 Sam. 25:3). She practiced the spirit of the third commandment.

About ten days later, Nabal got stiff as a board and died. Abigail became David's wife. And everybody praised God that they hadn't stooped to Nabal's level.

The lessons are so obvious that to spell them out almost steals their thunder. People are listening when we talk, and the dialogues we share are tuning us in to each other's soul. Our language tells what we're all about. May we, like Abigail, create zest and goodwill with our talk.

Nabal, like Hitler, began some big problems with his.

⑨ Secrecy

Private Disciple

Neither do people light a lamp and put it under a bowl. Instead they put it on its stand, and it gives light to everyone in the house (Matt. 5:15).

Write this epigram in neon. Make it big and bold and bright. Let it blink off and on. May the words be etched in the minds of every one of us: TRUTH IS OUTRAGED BY SILENCE.

Being an all-out disciple of Jesus Christ is a fearful thing. Because you and I both know that it brings a label. And, like most labels, it never tells the whole story. So some people become James Bond Christians—they go undercover!

Coming out of this closet is tough. I've been there. Near the end of my freshman year at Missouri University, I surrendered my life completely to Christ. I tolerated the rejection from campus kooks because only five weeks were left in the school year. Soon I would be home free. However, home meant facing Sam, my best friend. I knew I'd have to tell him up front about my decision.

Sure enough, shortly after I got back, Sam dropped by. We talked casually as we leaned against his blue Camaro—the same car in which we had often partied wildly, typical of teenagers without the Lord in their lives. I gradually worked up the courage to spill the beans.

When he asked me if I wanted to go have some beers, there was no way out. I looked him in the eye, swallowed hard, and said, "Sam, I can't. A few weeks ago I decided to follow God's will for my life. Jesus Christ is my Lord now."

That was one of the hardest things I've ever done. It grew silent. I could tell that Sam was embarrassed and didn't know what to say. My heart was pounding.

Finally I spoke up again: "I know this probably comes as a shocker to you." He nodded and smiled but still said nothing. "We've been friends for years," I added, "and that doesn't have to change. But I can't do the things I used to do anymore. Do you understand?"

He nodded and then replied, "I think that's fine for you. But I'm gonna do what I'm gonna do. And I guess that means we won't see each other much anymore."

Suddenly a barrier was between us. Nothing unfriendly, just tense. Then I said, "Well, I'm not saying you have to change. Just that when we're together, I don't want to do that stuff anymore."

He came back quickly and coolly: "That's up to you, I've got to go." He raced off. I knew then that we lived in different worlds and were headed in different directions. But when the chips were down, I couldn't play 007 with my faith.

Sad story. But what's that got to do with the third commandment? Sometimes secret disciples keep their cover by using profanity. The apostle Peter did. When he denied Jesus, Peter cursed and swore that he'd never even heard of Jesus (Matt. 26:74). Danger was glaring him in the face, and he traded his witness for safety. And it's so easy for us to sit back and fault Peter for being a coward.

The truth is, we've all stepped in his shoes. Like the time dirty jokes were flying around. Remember? Did you listen and laugh along, or did you walk away? Or like the time a few of your peers were cursing and ridiculing one of your "super-spiritual" classmates. Did you chime in, or did you defend the right one? Would people figure you to be a Christian by your language? Or is it possible that at times you have gone along with those who reviled God's name? Has your silence kept your faith a mystery?

Speaking up can be costly. After I told Sam about my decision, I didn't see him for a long time. In fact, it was over six years later. We ran into each other at a local shopping mall. Instantly his eyes grew wide, and we gave each other a bear hug. All we had shared could not be forgotten.

He was as excited to see me as I was to see him. "I've got something to tell you!" he grinned.

It struck me immediately. I blurted out, "You accepted Christ!"

"Yes! I did! I'm married now, and my wife has accepted Christ, too."

"That's wonderful," I said and put my arm around his shoulder as we walked.

"We enjoy church, and we read our Bible together," Sam added. He had the joy only Christians know.

The friendship was restored. And it also had an added dimension: fellowship. The barrier between us had become a bridge. Finally the price I had paid beside the blue Camaro was paying back dividends. At the moment of rejection, I thought I had been too blunt, and the loss was hard. But in the light of eternity, I'm glad I didn't play James Bond with my faith.

So the sad story has a happy ending. Not always, though. There's no sense in us pat-a-caking the issue. Refusing to join in with the foul-mouthed and evildoers is no guarantee that all of them will eventually run to Jesus. Some of them never will. Still, practicing the Praise Commandment is worth it.

Besides, silence is just the flip side of profanity. Both of them outrage the truth.

4

The Mellow Commandment

"Remember the Sabbath day by keeping it holy. Six days you shall labor and do all your work, but the seventh day is a Sabbath to the LORD your God. On it you shall not do any work, neither you, nor your son or daughter, nor your manservant or maidservant, nor your animals, nor the alien within your gates. For in six days the LORD made the heavens and the earth, the sea, and all that is in them, but he rested on the seventh day. Therefore the LORD blessed the Sabbath day and made it holy" (Exod. 20:8–11).

10 Relaxation

Gentle on My Mind

"Come to me, all you who are weary and burdened, and I will give you rest. Take my yoke upon you and learn from me, for I am gentle and humble in heart, and you will find rest for your souls. For my yoke is easy and my burden is light" (Matt. 11:28–30).

An Assyrian tablet of 200 B.C. says: "God does not subtract/From the allotted span of men's lives/the hours spent in fishing."

If that were true, one could live forever by fishing continuously. Some people might like to do that, but not me. The sport is fun enough; it's the worms I can't take! What a grizzly chore—sliding a worm on a hook! Making a big catch is a blast, though. There's something about a fighting fish that injects adrenaline into the bloodstream like racing fuel. Pure frenzy.

But get this: that's not why most fisherman fish. Genuine anglers don't haul out their gear, boats, waders, and stink bait just for the electric moment of snaring a five-pounder. Why, then? Because they love the outdoors . . . the smell of the water . . . the wisps of fog that hover at sunrise . . . the simple idleness of getting away . . . the distant cries of the bobwhite and whippoorwill at night. It isn't the catch that's important; it's the escape.

I doubt if God gives bonus time to people just for fishing. But I also doubt if he is pleased with those who drive themselves slavishly seven days a week. God is not into laziness, nor is he into drudgery. That's the message of the fourth commandment.

Jesus himself knew when to take a break. At times the crowds were so demanding and the days so tiring that Jesus needed a breather. Once he was so busy that there was no time to eat, and he turned to his disciples and ". . . said to them, 'Come with me by yourselves to a quiet place and get some rest' " (Mark 6:31).

On another occasion he tried to hide out at a friend's home to avoid the commotion that followed him. Mark 7:24 says it was in the city of Tyre. An appropriate place to relax, don't you agree?

Of all that can be studied about Jesus, Matthew 15:29 reveals one of my favorite things about him: "Jesus left there and went along the Sea of Galilee. Then he went up into the hills and sat down." Let the gentleness of that touch you for a while.

Jesus liked to walk barefoot on a sandy beach. He liked the dull roar of sea tides. He enjoyed the squish of wet sand between his toes. He felt soothed by the calls of the swooping gulls. Then he hiked up a mountain—Jesus often retreated into the mountains—and inhaled the thin fresh air of higher altitudes. That cool spot did something for him. It was like a transfusion of life. I love that about him.

He worked hard, too. He was consumed with ministry and lived as if every task was his most important. When the needy begged for his help, he sacrificed hours and days to serve them. There seemed to be no end to his energy, for it flowed from a heart rich with compassion. Each day, he spent himself completely. But he still knew when to step briefly aside from it all.

God rested on the seventh day for a reason. He could have created six-day weeks just as easily. Instead he singled out the last day. On that day he admired all that he had done. But more than that, he was setting an example for us to follow.

Let me ask you a question. Did God need the rest? I mean, was he wiped out by his long week of creating? Hardly. The rest was not for himself; it was for us. In essence God was saying, "Listen, it is good to know the meaning of rest; it is right to take pleasure in what you have accomplished; it is worthwhile to kick up your feet."

Originally it was a must that the Mellow Commandment was to be strictly observed: God was ordering everybody to take a day off. Later, under the New Covenant, Jesus pointed out the *spirit* of the Sabbath. He taught people how to take mini-Sabbaths. He also showed that the seventh day was not meant to be so rigid. An enforced rest day is ruined by no-exception rules and brings no rest.

The loose way in which Jesus approached the Sabbath really burned up the Pharisees, who said he defiled the spiritual day. But he had news for them! Check out Mark 2:27: "Then he said to them, 'The Sabbath was made for man, not man for the Sabbath. So the Son of Man is Lord even of the Sabbath.'"

Let me run that by you in the Earles paraphrase: "Then Jesus drove home the truth about the fourth commandment, 'Nobody knows better than I do how to act on the Sabbath, because I'm the One who started the day to begin with. So take five, guys!'"

For Christians the Sabbath has been replaced by the Lord's Day. It was chosen because Jesus resurrected on the first day of the week, signifying a new beginning. We need to rest because it strengthens us for a fresh start.

Ironically, what do you think Jesus did soon after his resurrection? Took his disciples fishing.

11 Recreation

Worlds of Fun

Command those who are rich in this present world not to be arrogant nor to put their hope in wealth, which is so uncertain, but to put their hope in God, who richly provides us with everything for our enjoyment (1 Tim. 6:17).

For a long time, one of the gripes against Christianity has been that it is so boring—dead, drab, humdrum. But is that a fair slap? Or is the actual complaint that the Bible labels drunkenness, illicit sex, cocaine sniffing, and such "unwholesome"?

I've been up front so far, so why back off now? I'm not going to erase the dividing line between righteousness and wickedness. People who want to play the prodigal will also learn the meaning of regret. Reckless living is not without its crashes. What a shame when a life becomes little more than scattered fragments. Who would celebrate anything that invites such disaster?

However, I must agree that some Christians are about as much fun as a wasp sting. If something is even remotely exciting, they're automatically against it. Anybody who does "wrong" (has a good time) is branded a rebel. These stoics give Christianity a bad name, and they leave a sour taste in the Lord's mouth. Pay them no mind.

An old hillbilly saying makes much better sense:

When I works, I works hard;
When I sits, I sits loose;
And when I thinks, I falls asleep.

God favors hard work, and he also approves of hard play. There are times, though, when the best recreation of all is sitting and falling asleep. Eventually you will come to appreciate that. Few things in life are as pleasurable as dozing off. O blessed nap!

Pardon me—I didn't mean to sound like a fuddy-duddy. I firmly believe that hard workers deserve the privilege of sitting loose. Nothing better expresses the pulsebeat of the Mellow Commandment than a good recliner. Believe it or not, God is not a glorified General Patton. Whoever started that rumor, anyway?

God laughs, you know. He does! Anybody who would recruit a bunch of guys like the twelve disciples would need a sense of humor to keep from going crazy! What's more, if *I* get tickled with *my* children, why should I think God is any different? He gets tickled with our antics, too. And I have to believe that God does not want us to miss out on having an occasional blast.

Here are some ideas to help make the good times better:

Really turn it loose. I bet you didn't expect to see that in a Christian book, did you? Well, there it is. No joke. Be crack-brained! To clarify, let me remind you that wickedness has no place in a Christian's lifestyle. Highs, hangovers, and harlotry are half-witted, and only fools call that fun. If such things are all you can come up with to do, you've got a lousy imagination. Take note of 1 Timothy 6:17, which expresses the New Testament spirit of the fourth commandment better: ". . . [God] richly provides us with everything for our enjoyment." You don't have to look beyond what's right to find something to do. Just be *holy* crazy!

Watch your circle. If it happened to the prodigal, it can happen to you. He wasn't careful about who he ran around with. Ungodly people would say he had a great time. He got drunk a lot, had a lot of women, gambled away loads of money, and was the life of the party. Until he ran out of dough. No bucks, no buddies. Everybody dropped him. That's the way of the worldly. The prodigal ended up eating pig slop—literally. Your circle of friends can be the difference between times you will always remember or times you wish you could forget! Think that over.

Throw down anchors. Creative pandemonium is all right occasionally, but life can't be an endless Chinese fire drill. All chaos must calm to order. If you never throw out an anchor and get down to business when necessary, you'll be lost at sea. Last time I heard, normal folks still have to study and work hard to become whatever it is they want to become. You may be tempted to be the ultimate goof-off during your first year out of high school, especially if you're still living with your family. If you move out on your own, the pressure may be even greater. So keep your anchors polished and use them wisely.

One last piece of advice. Sit loose.

12 Reflection

Spiritual Oil Change

Therefore we do not lose heart. Though outwardly we are wasting away, yet inwardly we are being renewed day by day (2 Cor. 4:16).

Five decades ago, T. S. Eliot wrote these pungent words: "Human kind cannot bear very much reality."

Here comes the other side of the Mellow Commandment that you may have been wondering if I'd mention. The Sabbath was meant to be more than a one-day vacation. Often our problem is that we play *too* much. From surfing to sailing to skiing, Americans usually need very little urging to frolic.

We like reality in small doses, and busyness keeps us from thinking. So we go, go, go. Whether it's working or playing, bustle means amnesia, our way of forgetting. Commandment number four puts a lid on that kettle. When Moses brought the seventh-day concept down from the mountain, it was to remind people to think. To muse. To chew their cud. To reflect.

Socrates once said, "The unexamined life is not worth living." Although we don't need to pick ourselves apart, spiritual health requires that we all do occasional soul-searching. For a brief time each week—on a rest day—it is good to get alone and lick our spiritual wounds.

After all, we have other checkups: medical and dental exams and visits to the eye doctor. Pest killers probe for bugs, and teachers give tests. Most homes get a weekly routine once-over to clear away the dust. Why, you probably even take better care of your car than you do your inner self.

Have you seen that sneering mechanic of TV-commercial fame? He talks about the serious business of regularly changing a car's oil filter. Quite nonchalant. Doesn't it just burn you up when he says, "Pay me now or pay me later"? His smirk is annoying, but he's still right. If the engine quits, what good is the car? Oil lubricates the engine. Clean oil—clean engine—smooth ride. Nice and simple.

Lift the hood of your spiritual life. Take a look. Low on oil? Oil dirty? Any knocks or pings? That's the purpose of reflection. Paul said it differently: ". . . inwardly we are being renewed day by day" (2 Cor. 4:16). But it means the same thing. REST spells recuperation and renewal.

Wise Christians do their own regular spiritual oil changes. They get higher output and better mileage. Added to that, there's less wear and tear on mind and body. How does that translate?

Lower risk for depression

Fewer temper tirades

Quicker response against temptation

Keener insight

More meaningful fellowship with Christ

Deeper prayer life

Joy you can feel

Although God doesn't take a "pay me now or pay me later" attitude toward us, a filthy spirit can be costly. Check these symptoms of "engine" trouble *before* you blow a gasket:

Irregular running. It is not normal for a car to jerk with convulsions. Those of us with jalopies are used to it. Still, that's no way to run a life. If you are hot one day and cold the next, you need the Mellow Commandment. If you have lots of spiritual ups and downs, check your spark plugs. Ask yourself what motivates you. Examine your heart. Pinpoint what is distracting you and causing your stop-and-go lifestyle. Do something about it. Or else your engine will die.

Unusual smoke. Careless Christians like to kid themselves into believing they're invincible. "Put the pedal to the metal" is their motto. Result? Burnout. Like the case of the "overnight apostle." These types try to memorize their Bible in two hours, win three thousand souls to Christ with one sermon, and conquer the devil with one punch. They usually become casualties themselves. The worst smoke of all is in kidding yourself that everything will be okay if you travel at high speeds. Grow at a normal pace. Christ was born in Bethlehem, not Indianapolis.

Excessive leaks. Nothing signals a sick car like three inches of ooze on your garage floor. Leaks mean your engine is hurting. Pain. Most of our spiritual leakage comes out of our eyes. Or perhaps as senseless, emotional babbling from our mouths. Constant leaking indicates a need for rest. Sort of a Sabbath. A chance to lean back into the arms of the Lord. With cars, leaks are bad news; with Christians, it can be a time of cleansing. But if the power of the Holy Spirit seeps out, you're going to crack a piston.

The man in the oil-filter commercial makes good sense. But I still don't like his smirk. Too much reality.

5

The Maturity Commandment

"Honor your father and your mother, so that you may live long in the land the LORD your God is giving you" (Exod. 20:12).

13 Respect

Manner of Tact

Show proper respect to everyone: Love the brotherhood of believers, fear God, honor the king (1 Peter 2:17).

Ages five and six were painful for me. It was then that I began acting like a moron. Huckleberry Finn would have been shocked to see this brat at work. It was also then that my parents "urged" me to become a decent little kid. That was the painful part. They used a firm hand on my sit-down-area to trounce the barbarian in me.

The Turnip Raid was my first great crime. Our back yard was very long, and it was bordered on the far-left corner by Mr. Early's garden. A tool shed hid the garden from the view of both our house and the Earlys'. One summer afternoon I sat on the bank beside the horticulturist's masterpiece, admiring the well-weeded rows. An idea promptly hit me: "Why not yank up a few vegetables and give them a try?"

Visions of raw turnips danced in my head. The dirt was so loamy that I had no problem heisting a good load of big juicy turnips. Anything much smaller than a baseball I just threw in the gravel road that circled out back. To complete my felony, I washed off the turnips with Mr. Early's garden hose, scraped off the tart skins with my pocket knife, and munched down. After I had eaten my fill, I casually tossed the remains back into the garden.

That night I got my first lesson in respect.

Once I had recovered enough to forget lesson number one, I committed my second great crime. You may not have heard of the Rock Massacre of '62, but I shall never forget it. At the far edge of our back yard, across from Mr. Early's garden, was our garage. It was convenient to the gravel road that wound around. I loved rocks: throwing them, hitting them, breaking things with them.

Dad's garage was almost as much window as wood. Furthermore, each window was made up of many small individual panes. You guessed it—I knocked out every single one! Mom caught me in the act of this savage outrage. All she could say was, "I'm going to tell your dad, and he is going to kill you!" I don't know how many times she said that, but I lost count after one hundred.

That night I got my second lesson in respect.

This time my recovery was much slower. Still, it did not prevent my worst crime of all: the Great Nun Caper. My dad had ordered a catalog item that came delivered in a hollow bamboo rod. The rod became my newest toy—and a dangerous weapon! It made the perfect slingshot. Still stricken with a rock fetish, I would load the bamboo machine gun and zap my target with primitive explosives. A rock bath.

About a block up the street was a convent. One day, when I was practicing with my war gun, a bunch of nuns set out for the grocery store. Another brilliant idea struck me: "What would it be like to blast a passing car?" Destiny would have it that the good sisters were in the next car to come by. One busted windshield later, I heard my mom's famous words again: "Your dad is going to kill you!"

That night I got my third lesson in respect.

By now you're probably wondering what kept me from becoming the next John Dillinger. It was Dad's spankings. Having to deal with his hands-on application after every disrespectful act saved me.

But respect means more than good behavior. Respect involves words, expressions, and attitude. It is knowing how and when to be kind. It is recognizing what to do and what not to do. It is learning to treat friend and enemy alike. It is not as much forced as it is un-practiced and natural. Respect is the offspring of obedience.

And from where does such a quality come? The Maturity Commandment holds the key. Children learn it through the discipline and teaching given by their parents. Sometimes it's a spanking or other punishment. Sometimes it's a lecture. Sometimes it's a story from yesteryear (i.e., "Well, when I was your age. . ."). Sometimes it's a mean glare. But all along, respect is being taught.

God knew that if we learned to respect our parents, it would be easy to learn respect for others. If we cannot honor them, we will be disrespectful to everyone else. The rebel who never matures, who never stops being dishonorable, ends up a huge mess.

Like Hophni and Phinehas. Who? Eli's sons. Check the Old Testament in 1 Samuel, chapters 2 and 4. Those guys were an embarrassment to their old dad. And it caught up with them. Listen to what God had to say:

> [A man of God said to Eli,] "Therefore the LORD, the God of Israel, declares: . . . 'And what happens to your two sons, Hophni and Phinehas, will be a sign to you—they will both die on the same day. I will raise up for myself a faithful priest, who will do according to what is in my heart and mind . . .'" (1 Sam. 2:30, 34–35).

God wanted men who were respectful, not a couple of meatheads. Hophni and Phinehas had never learned to please their dad. As a result, they were unable to please God, or anybody else for that matter. A short time later the wicked sons died a tragic death to match the kind of life they had lived. When Eli heard of their death, he had a heart attack, fell off his chair, broke his neck, and died.

Phinehas's wife was pregnant. The awful news sent her into labor. When her son was born, she named him Ichabod, or "no God." The name means: "The glory of God has departed." Read the whole sad story in 1 Samuel 4:1–22.

Principle: God's glory always departs when respect is nowhere to be found. Respect is a matter of maturity. It is finally pooling all childhood lessons into one sensible pile. And seeing that the pieces belong to one picture, each jagged piece falling into place with the others. The meaning is complete: I owe to God, myself—and all people—the dignity of being the best I can be.

Anything less is Ichabod.

The Great Nun Caper taught me that.

14 Home

Blessing or Battleground?

But if a widow has children or grandchildren, these should learn first of all to put their religion into practice by caring for their own family and so repaying their parents and grandparents, for this is pleasing to God (1 Tim. 5:4).

Statistics. Ugh! Numerical lists make me tired. Since a cunning person can use them to prove almost anything, I wonder how many of them are really worthwhile. That's a clever way of setting you up for yet another list. Except this time the numbers warn us to take inventory. In finding these facts, I was forced to ponder the fate of our country's home life if the trend continues. Since you will be building tomorrow's families, I thought it necessary to let you in on what's brewing.

- 18 percent of all births are to unmarried mothers, and 50 percent of those are to teenagers.
- As many as 60 percent of newborns will spend time in single-parent homes.
- 250,000 children are physically abused every year. Nearly 100,000 of those are also sexually abused.

Child abuse is the leading cause of death for children *under the age of five*!

Over 30 percent of all homes experience other forms of abuse or violence.

Approximately 15 million women are battered by their husbands every year. That figure is probably too low, since most such beatings go unreported.

Slightly less than half of all first-time marriages end in divorce. Most of those people will remarry, and half will divorce again.

Suicide is the ultimate barbiturate in American homes. Thousands of teenagers kill themselves each year. But it is almost as popular with the 18–24 age group. Americans—the people with the greatest hope of opportunity in the world—are checking out by the dozens every day.

Complicate all of that with drug and/or alcohol abuse. Throw in several thousand domestic murders every year. Pile on hundreds of runaways. Don't forget the cases of entire families abandoned by one of the parents. Tally in the toll of the loose philosophy that says to "live together because marriage is old-fashioned." Keep in mind today's working women and the effect this is having on the family. Because—like it or not—it is having some repercussions. Another straw on the camel's back is that too many families are torn by hatred, where one of the kids has not spoken to his or her parents for months, maybe even years.

Enough is enough. That should sufficiently drill into your head the conditions in families and homes across our country. I have neither long speeches on how we got this bad off nor pat answers on how to get out of this mess. But I think a lot of our problems began when we starting shucking the fifth commandment. Now, instead of the family being a caring unit, it is in need of a CARE unit. The paramedics are you!

One or two good crops of solid families could get us started back on the right track. Otherwise, HOME is likely to become an ugly four-letter word, if you get my drift. For hundreds of thousands, it is already so terrible that they have confused it with HELL, the four-letter word that HOME is on its way to becoming.

What shall we do? Loud-mouthed critics say, "Let the ship sink. She isn't fit for our age of free lifestyles."

"Bah, humbug!" you say (I hope). Hold your britches. They have a point. If we plan to be wild and free, then perhaps we should let the once-honored home join the *Titanic*. After all, these statistics are real, and they're not going to go away on their own. People like yourself are going to have to use your brains and energy. It takes guts to shoulder the responsibility of developing a meaningful family life. There's just no room for a "don't fence me in" mentality. "Home" happens when two people settle in for a long lifetime of teamwork, sweat, godliness, and prayer—to carry on the fine tradition of the fifth commandment.

The New Testament adds a slant on this commandment that is being forgotten in our day. In 1 Timothy 5:4 we are told to care for our parents and grandparents when they become feeble and helpless. That is our chance to repay them for changing our dirty diapers, buying our clothes, paying our doctor and dentist bills, sending us to college, and everything else they have done for us. The Maturity Commandment still applies throughout all of life.

I hope all my grim statistics haven't scared you away from having a family, because there are still millions of terrific families in our country. If you've been blessed enough to be part of one, then you know how wonderful it can be. If not, then you have the incentive to change things so that you, too, will be able to experience the joys of a happy home life.

Each of us has things we love most about home: the sound of genuine, uncensored laughter or music that soothes the soul, for example. The sight of children playing and the toys that remind us of our own childhood. Knowing that there are at least a few people who accept you as you are. Feeling secure. Having people to share your heart and burdens. Crazy family games. Prayer time together. Simple quietness and the ticking of the living-room clock. Someone to hug. Someone to tell "I love you," and someone who will say it back. The refrigerator. The cookie jar. The coffee pot. Clean sheets and warm blankets. The family pet. I could go on, but you have your own list.

You don't want to miss that. Believe me, it just keeps getting better. For those who work at it.

For those who don't . . . Well, they become part of the nauseating statistics.

15 Independence
Putting Away Childish Things

> *When I was a child, I talked like a child, I thought like a child, I reasoned like a child. When I became a man, I put childish ways behind me* (1 Cor. 13:11).

My son, Jared, is five years old. His sparkling innocence has often supplied our household with a cute moment to remember. Recently, upon giving his mother a big hug and kiss, he proudly announced, "Mommy, when I grow up, I'm going to marry you." All little boys say that before they're old enough to know how prime the field gets at age sixteen. A little girl says the same thing to her daddy.

Back to Jared. Of course, Jane and I held back our laughter, pleased with his simple show of love. "Well, son, that's very nice, but I'm already married to your daddy," came Jane's light-hearted response.

"Oh," he paused. "Well can't I marry you, too?"

"I'll be too old to marry by the time you grow up," she said as I listened in.

"Oh!" He seemed almost devastated, then fired back, "Okay, I'll marry Sara!" Sara is his three-year-old sister.

It seemed like a good time for me to join in, so I said, "Son, you can't marry your sister."

He asked the question I expected: "Why not?"

"Because it doesn't work that way. When you become a young man, there will be hundreds of beautiful girls to choose from. You will fall in love with one of them, and that is whom you will want to marry."

His reply was a classic: "Are you trying to tell me not to be in such a big hurry?"

Stunned by his insight, the best I could muster was a shrug and a calm "Yes." Again, a five-year-old had uncovered a great truth: we spend half of our lives wishing the other half would come.

Do you remember how, as a child, you wondered if you'd ever grow up? First you thought you'd never be old enough to go to school. Then, after you found out how much "fun" school is, you thought you would never get out. You waited "forever" to get your license and take the car for a spin by yourself. Almost "a million years" passed before your first date finally arrived. Each of the years after your twelfth birthday had ten thousand days. The only thing that kept you together was the dream that one day you might graduate. Suddenly it's here!

You don't talk so much like a child anymore. Your thoughts are not nearly as naive and immature as they once were. Childish ideals of life have faded into youthful zeal and plain reality. Even yesterday's toys have been replaced.

I am reminded of an incident that Dr. James Dobson shared in his best-selling book, *Straight Talk to Men and Their Wives.* He writes:

Our daughter, especially, has loved every aspect of childhood and has been most reluctant to leave it. Her phonograph records and her stuffed animals and her bedroom have been prized possessions since toddlerhood. Likewise, she sat on Santa's lap for four years after she knew he was a phony. But, alas, she turned thirteen years old and began hearing a new set of drums. About a year ago, she went through her toys and records, stacking them neatly and leaving them in front of Ryan's bedroom door. On the top was a note which Shirley brought to me with tears in her eyes. It read:

Dear Ryan:

These are yours now.
Take good care of them
like I have.

Love, Danae

That brief message signaled the closing of the door called "Childhood." And once it shut, no power on earth could open it again. . . .*

You are now standing at the threshold of the doorway called "Adulthood." It took a long time to get here, but perhaps you are not as ready for it as you once thought. Nothing will be the same again.

Normally I don't like to be bossy. But humor me for a second. Chances are that you and your parents have had some pretty tense run-ins during these last few years. While you have been trying to spread your wings, they have been Johnny-on-the-spot to clip them. No doubt some pecking and snapping has left the nest a bit messy. Now it is the time to start straightening things up.

Don't start off on your own with a mad-at-your-parents attitude, even if they were wrong about some things. Self-righteously flaunting independence doesn't make an adult out of anyone. Don't feel as if you have to prove to them that now you can do whatever you want. Good grief, that's a throwback to childishness.

If you think growing up has been tough on you, well, it's been hard on them, too. So give them the same break that you want from them. Stay levelheaded and they will gradually let you go. It will be one of the hardest things they have ever done. But they know they must.

And so must you. Kids sometimes cling more than their parents do. Independence is scary, so they want to taste it only in small bites. If you're still holding on, now is the time to turn loose. Just unbend your fingers and let childhood fall from your hands. You

*From *Straight Talk to Men and Their Wives* by Dr. James C. Dobson, copyright © 1980; used by permission of Word Books, Publisher, Waco, Texas 76796.

might feel empty-handed, but you'll be full-hearted. Memories last forever. Cry if you want to. I did.

Then, when you get married, the whole process will start again. In reverse.

The Temper Commandment

"You shall not murder" (Exod. 20:13).

16 Jealousy

Keeper of the Dragon

You are still worldly. For since there is jealousy and quarreling among you, are you not worldly? Are you not acting like mere men? (1 Cor. 3:3).

An old proverb has it that "jealousy feeds upon suspicion, and it turns into fury." When God catalogued sin in Galatians 5:19–21, he indexed jealousy alongside such things as hatred, discord, fits of rage, selfish ambition, dissention, factions, and envy.

But doesn't the Bible say that even God gets jealous? you might be thinking. Yes, it does. God *is* jealous of his children; he doesn't want us dividing our time and love between him and other gods. However, I think it is important to understand that God's jealousy is totally opposite of the evil form of jealousy we are accustomed to seeing in humans. Perhaps Joshua 24:19 pinpoints it best: "... He is a holy God; he is a jealous God. . . ." God's jealousy is described in the same breath with his holiness. In other words, it is not sinful suspicion he feels toward unfaithful followers; it is holy affection. Paul expressed it perfectly when he said, "I am jealous for you with a godly jealousy. . ." (2 Cor. 11:2). Godly jealousy harbors no selfish feelings. It is based on what is loving, pure, and right, not hurt, anger, and distrust.

It is possible for us to feel a proper and acceptable form of jealousy. A husband who protects his wife from flirtatious goons is not doing wrong. A wife who gives a warning look to a husband-chaser is practicing godly jealousy. A pastor who prevents flower-selling cult members from sneaking into his congregation is right on track.

But wait. Most jealousy is not like that. The green-eyed dragon we shelter breathes no noble fires. He harms the fine princess; he doesn't rescue her. Mere human jealousy usually runs amuck, burning the whole countryside to a crisp. He is a vicious beast, easy to spot because of his four heads, each of which has a name that begins with *R*.

Resentment. Hidden huffiness is the first head. Watch as it grinds its teeth and quivers with fury. So mad it could spit, its fumes of bitterness burst into flames when they are ignited by the fear of being slighted.

Grab your Bible. Flip to Genesis 37:11. Jacob's sons were jealous of their brother, Joseph. They resented him. He was bright, handsome, and a good dresser. Daddy liked him best because he came from the favorite wife, Rachel, so the brothers boiled with bitterness when he came around. To make it worse, the kid was a likable young gentleman.

One day Jake sent little Joe out to see how his older brothers were doing with the sheep. Genesis 37:18 says, "But they saw him in the distance, and before he reached them, they plotted to kill him." Wow! Talk about drastic! Kill him? Innocent as jealous resentment seems, it is a violation of the Temper Commandment. Jealousy is quite capable of murder.

Joseph got off easy. They stole his fancy robe, threw him in a ditch, and sold him as a slave to the Ishmaelites. Nice family. If you think they didn't break the sixth commandment, then you don't have a handle on the spirit of what it says.

Rivalry. Still got your Bible? Go back a few pages to Genesis 30. Here is the story of two sisters who were jealous of each other—Rachel and Leah. Their jealousy grew into competition. They would stop at nothing to outdo the other. This is one of the most shameful narratives in Scripture. Read it for yourself. I'm too nauseated to tell it.

The dragon's second head hates being number two. It will strive and manipulate to knock off any opponent. Rivalry has been known to split families and friendships. What an expense for the privilege of outdoing someone!

Can you be happy for someone who received recognition that you did not? How do you feel toward a competitor who has accomplished what you have not? Do you look upon people as "enemies" if they are succeeding when you are failing? When you do have to compete, do you have a "kill" attitude? Remember that neither Rachel nor Leah lived a truly happy life.

Revenge. The third head of jealousy was once worn by King Saul. After David plastered Goliath, all the townsfolk gathered for a ticker-tape parade. Young Dave rode in the main chariot, and all the people went berserk over the wonder boy. "And from that time on Saul kept a jealous eye on David" (1 Sam. 18:9).

Saul's son, Jonathan, became best friends with David. Dad looked at their friendship through green-colored glasses, and the jealousy drove a wedge between him and his son. Things got so out of hand that Saul tried to kill David. More than once! In fact, when the priests of Nob sided with David, the ruthless king had them slaughtered (1 Sam. 22:17–20). Eighty-five men of God were murdered because of jealousy!

Why Saul wanted revenge really doesn't make any sense. David did no wrong to Saul. Was it his fault that he was well-liked and the king was rejected? He didn't try to shame Saul or intentionally hurt him. Saul just had a character flaw. That's all. He was so full of self that he was willing to kill anybody who got in his way. David was innocent, but Saul pronounced him guilty. The hunt was on. Such is the way of a dragon.

Rage. The fourth head exhales the hottest flames. And out of its nose comes the vilest smoke. No other aspect has a greater potential of becoming nuclear than temper. Proverbs 27:4 says, "Anger is cruel and fury overwhelming, but who can stand before jealousy?"

Violence results when a person is completely out of control with rage. The aftermath resembles a tornado's destruction. "Things" can be replaced or fixed, though. Hearts cannot. All violence is not physical. Rage is on-the-heart attack. It aches to humiliate "the enemy."

When the dragon of jealousy gets loose, one or all of his four heads will be aroused. He takes no prisoners. And he leaves only victims. But none is so burned as the jealous one. The green-eyed dragon took Saul to his grave.

17 Hatred

Helter Skelter

[*Jesus taught:*] *"You have heard that it was said, 'Love your neighbor and hate your enemy.' But I tell you: Love your enemies and pray for those who persecute you"* (Matt. 5:43–44).

Number 10050 Cielo Drive was a quiet, secluded spot. It was in a neighborhood with ideal privacy for the elite of Bel Air, California. But on August 9th and 10th of 1969, Cielo Drive became the stage for one of modern history's most bizarre crimes. Down the street at 10070 Cielo Drive, the neighbors heard faint cries shortly after midnight that early August. They said it sounded as if a woman was begging for mercy, crying, "Oh, God! No! Don't, please don't, don't, don't, don't. . . ." But there were no loud screams. No unusual noises. No other cries besides those that were only barely audible. Then 10050 Cielo Drive went back to its usual silent self. Or did it?

The grotesque massacre found later by police officers was horrifying and beyond human comprehension. One officer said that "it was unimaginable that someone could do such things to another human being." Corpses lay in the yard, no doubt slaughtered while trying to escape. The house smelled of blood and death. Bodies were scattered. The silence was eerie. Who would do this? And why?

Pools of blood were everywhere. The victims had been shot, stabbed, and bludgeoned. Blood had been smeared all over the dead bodies. One woman had the word WAR carved on her stomach, and PIG had been written on the wall in blood. The world sat in utter shock that innocent people could be so brutally butchered and killed. Little had the residents on Cielo Drive known that the cries they had heard *were* the cries of a woman begging—for her life.

Charles Manson and his "family" were the ones responsible for the gory nightmare known as the Sharon Tate-LaBianca murders. Eventually they were proven guilty of this unthinkable bloodbath. During their trial, one of the young women who had killed Sharon Tate and her baby said, "You really have to love people to do something like that for them." Chilling, isn't it? But nothing described the savage acts as fully as the bloody words painted on the refrigerator door—HELTER SKELTER.

"Psychopaths!" you say. "Lunatics! Maniacs!" You're right. Only an insane, crazed animal could do such mad things. And yet even this inhuman extreme began as hatred, an all-too-human emotion. Regardless of any other motive for murder, hatred has a part in it all. That is what makes hatred so dangerous. So it is an awful sin.

Is it ever okay to hate? Well, I don't know about you, but there are some things I *hate*. Disliking them is not enough. I hate them! Like snakes. I hate snakes! All snakes! I don't care what anybody says, I detest the creepy crawlers. And don't tell me about harmless little garden snakes. I'd as soon kill them as look at them. Even if you turn me in to the Reptile Protection Society, if there is one, I'll be a snake-hating, snake-killing fanatic till the day I die.

I hate flies, too. They buzz around. They tickle you when they walk on your skin. They get on the TV screen when you're trying to watch your favorite program. They play in the yuckiest places and then come and put their feet on your food. They sneak under your lampshade when you're trying to read at night and bounce around, making distracting thumping noises. They're ugly. You have to hate them. And you have to kill them. It's like the Code of the West.

Crabgrass was made to hate. When you get your own lawn, you'll know exactly what I'm talking about. The stuff is a yard hog. It takes over everything, drinks all the water, chokes out all the other grass. It gets in your flowerbeds and smothers your petunias. And mortar fire is the only thing that kills it. I don't dislike crabgrass; I hate it.

Watches that have alarms—now there is something I really hate. Have you ever been in a roomful of people, each wearing one of those annoying clocks, which were all set to beep at the same time? I have! No two watches were in synch, meaning that every watch started beeping at a different moment. The result was two or three minutes' worth of weird noises reminiscent of a clock shop. I wanted to rip off the noisy wrist-beepers and crush their cute little faces into cement. If you've got one of those menaces to society, keep the pesky thing away from me. Or else it will need a watch doctor.

The Bible affirms that hatred is perfectly normal in some instances. Amos 5:15 tells us to "hate evil, love good. . . ." The psalmist said, ". . . I hate every wrong path" (Ps. 119:128). When Wisdom speaks in Proverbs 8:13, it proclaims, "To fear the Lord is to hate evil; I hate pride and arrogance, evil behavior and perverse speech." And Ecclesiastes reminds us that there is "a time to love and a time to hate. . ." (3:8).

However, Jesus was very clear—we are never to hate *people*. Even enemies should not be hated. We should pray for those who use us or take advantage of us. When people mistreat us or abuse us, we should ask God to deal with them, and we should ask him to give us a heart free from bitterness. That isn't easy. Because none of us likes being walked on. Nobody wants to be a doormat. Right?

Well, then, why did Jesus give us a follow-up to the sixth commandment like Matthew 5:43–44? Does he just expect us to get kicked around and take it? No. It's not at all like that. Of course we can defend ourselves. But our defense should not become offensive. I mean "offensive" as in B.O. Our words and actions toward enemies should never be cruel, revengeful, or filled with hate. That stinks.

Before people come to Christ, they play hating games—". . . being hated and hating one another" (Titus 3:3). But once they accept the Lord's kindness, love, and mercy, they do not return an eye for an eye, or hate for hate. They learn to inhale the life-breath of the Temper Commandment:

. . . for it is written . . .

"If your enemy is hungry, feed him;
if he is thirsty, give him something to drink.
In doing this, you will heap burning coals on his head."

Do not be overcome by evil, but overcome evil with good (Rom. 12:19–21).

Unfortunately the world as we know it will always be infested with spite and hostility. O that hatred would never touch anything more significant than snakes, flies, crabgrass, and beeping watches. We can be sure, though, that a world that hated Jesus Christ enough to thrust him upon a cross will not suddenly stop shedding blood today. Some people like their hate; it's all they have to keep them warm.

But let us not forget what hatred can become. The haunting chill of 10050 Cielo Drive begs us to remember.

18 Tolerance

No Jacket Required

Accept him whose faith is weak, without passing judgment on disputable matters (Rom. 14:1).

Jonathan Swift, the satirical author of *Gulliver's Travels,* said, "We have just enough religion to make us hate, but not enough to make us love one another."

Wham! Did he ever hit the nail on the head! Sure, the sixth commandment is talking about literal murder, but there are other ways of "killing" people. Like verbal torture, pitiless rejection, harsh criticism, and cruel insensitivity. How blind we can be to the deep wounds left by a tyrant spirit. They hurt as much as bullets, but all of the bleeding is internal. And though the body does not die, in many ways the *person* does.

I can hear you now: "C'mon, Earles, are you trying to tell me that everybody's easy to get along with? Some people are just a bit hard to take!" Okay, I get your point. You're right, we can't expect every human being to act like a human. But what are we going to do with the unbearable Darth Vader types? Strike them with our light saber? Bomb them with a thermonuclear detonator?

An anonymous ditty has it: "To live above with saints we love,/O that will be glory;/To dwell below with saints we know,/Now that's a different story!"

If that weren't so true, it would be funny. Don't get me wrong: ungodly people can be pretty hard to accept—but Christians have a special knack for biting on one another. The way brothers and sisters slap and fuss and feud goes on in God's family, too. I'm not excusing it, but just trying to warn you that some of the meanest characters in town are supposed to be Christians.

Captain Intolerance wrote these lines. Didn't sign his name. It's just as well. He speaks for so many:

> Believe as I believe—no more, no less;
> That I am right (and no one else) confess.
> Feel as I feel, think only as I think;
> Eat what I eat, and drink but what I drink.
> Look as I look, do always as I do;
> And then—and only then—I'll fellowship with you.

Listen, we expect way too much of each other. And we send fellow Christians on more than enough guilt trips. Why don't we stop being a bunch of knotheads and start accepting one another for what we are—humans who blow it every now and then. Deal?

"All right, but how am I supposed to tolerate somebody who could be a stand-in for J. R. Ewing?" you ask. That's a tough one. Actually, though, tolerance has some main ingredients that can always blend into a fine recipe for peace. And they can help you keep your temper, too:

Consider yourself. Yuk! This part doesn't taste good at all. It's like baking soda or onion powder. But Jesus really harped on it when he said:

> "Why do you look at the speck of sawdust in your brother's eye and pay no attention to the plank in your own eye? How can you say to your brother, 'Let me take the speck out of your eye,' when all the time there is a plank in your own eye? You hypocrite, first take the plank out of your own eye, and then you will see clearly to remove the speck from your brother's eye" (Matt. 7:3–5).

Some sermon, huh? Bet you never realized Jesus felt so strongly on the issue. His point deserves to be first on the list: when looking in the mirror, we find others easier to accept.

Remember forgiveness. When God forgave our sins and accepted us, he showed a great deal more tolerance than we'll ever show. Nonetheless, shouldn't we also be forgiving? With a merciful heart, couldn't we overlook the faults of those who make us crazy? I'm not suggesting that we applaud sinful living. But must we cast stones at those who fall short of our requirements? Remember: even Jesus ate with sinners.

Show kindness. Tolerance is more than dreaded endurance, although I must admit that an hour with some people is a lot like a ten-kilometer run. Exhaustion sets in after about fifteen minutes. "Enduring" people is harder than being kind to them, believe it or not. Why? Because being kind is a positive act and makes you feel better. You don't go away feeling like a rat for being passive and rude. It was Ben Franklin who said, "When you are good to others, you are best to yourself." Don't just endure people, be kind to them.

I'm glad that God is not as nit-picky as we are. If he were like us, he'd be throwing fireballs down from heaven all of the time. We're too much like James and John. Remember their nickname? Sons of Thunder. Whenever people didn't measure up to their standard, they wanted God to scorch them real good. They actually wanted them killed! (Luke 9:51–56). See how far intolerance will go?

Jonathan Swift, maybe you're right.

7

The Virtue Commandment

*"You shall not commit adultery"
(Exod. 20:14).*

19 Sex

For Adults Only

But if they cannot control themselves, they should marry, for it is better to marry than to burn with passion (1 Cor. 7:9).

Sex can be wholesome fun! That has to come as a relief to you. Because, since you've been old enough to understand sex jokes, you've been conditioned to believe that there's something dirty about lovemaking. Television and Hollywood have not exactly painted a clean picture. Porno magazines are geared only to intoxicate our hot animal magnetism, which gives off the impression that all sexuality is cheap. The upsweep of rape and other brutal sex crimes has burned an ugly image into the back of our minds: that sex is violent and, for women, painful. Advertising, with its careful portrayal of mouth-watering flesh, hints that body heat is a powerful tool we can use to get our way. All in all, sex has become such a popular subject, and we have heard so much about it, that we have been left with the feeling that it is negative and bad, if not boring.

When some *Christians* talk about sex, it isn't the Victorian, hush-hush topic that it was years ago. Instead, they now make it sound as if angels are supposed to sing in the background when a husband and wife are intimate. The spiritual aspect of intercourse has been preached until we've gotten the idea that the bedroom is the sanctuary of the home, with the bed as the altar. Blah! Let's not "religionize" lovemaking just because the world is trashing up what God intended for pleasure.

Pleasure? I thought that might catch you by surprise. Not only is sex supposed to be fun, but it's also meant to be sumptuous and gratifying. But God's wise requirement for the one-flesh relationship is marriage. Sex is a by-product of love and marriage, and neither is a playground, although both partners find their paradise in marital union. Once a couple obeys the boundary line, choosing to honor God, then the fireworks are ready to begin. No kidding! I'm not going to play cutsie, hide-and-seek games with you. (I assume you recall we are discussing the Virtue Commandment.) Solomon urged his son to have a good time with his wife. Let's listen in:

> "... and may you rejoice in the wife of your youth. A loving doe, a graceful deer—may her breasts satisfy you always, may you ever be captivated by her love. Why be captivated, my son, by an adulteress? Why embrace the bosom of another man's wife?" (Prov. 5:18–20).

It only makes sense that anything said to the sons also went vice versa for the daughters. What's good for the goose is good for the gander.

Extramarital sex, though, is nothing more than an ego trip. People in our culture crave to be noticed and chased by the opposite sex. It turns them on to entice each other; it makes them feel important. Some people like sexual flings because they get their jollies out of knowing they have the musk that attracts lovers. Having many different sexual partners is the way they feed their lust to control another person. Then, after the fruit has been eaten, they go back on the prowl for another sucker.

Silly girls are usually naive about this. They don't realize that they mean nothing to the bed-hoppers they play with. While a young woman may look upon the romp as love, the Romeo is adding another scalp to his collection. And in our permissive day, there are probably some loose ladies who run the same con.

When I say that sex ought to be fun and pleasurable, I'm talking about love of another kind. For one thing, it's fun when the play-mates *belong* to each other. It's enjoyable when they have a well-rounded marriage that doesn't depend upon sex to be the glue that holds it all together. It's delectable when they take time to tease and stimulate each other to the max. It's blissful when they are un-inhibited, realizing they have nothing to be ashamed of. It sparkles when they don't expect each love session to outdo the last. Sex is its very best when the two partners can be open and share and laugh, knowing that God made them to be together. When all of these in-gredients blend into one, sexual love is holy.

Adultery kills that. Premarital sex steals from the magic. Homo-sexuality mocks and humiliates the act and the partners. God knew these facts. And that is why he carved the seventh commandment into stone. The whole point of the commandment was to safeguard the individual from making sex into a toy. Not just to protect mar-riage, but to protect people from heartbreak! You see, when fun goes wild, pain is on the way.

Maybe you've been fantasizing lately and wondering whether you are, as someone put it, "one of the devil's angels, with sex where your brains ought to be." Well, I'm glad to hear that you're normal. If the topic did not interest you, then a visit to a psychiatrist would be in order.

You know what bugs me? It bothers me that young people today are made to feel guilty about their sexuality. Please don't look upon your wait for God's timing as merely "the legal process." See it as his way of preparing you for a lifetime of experimenting with the same person, in mutual love and commitment. And when you finally get your mate, don't be afraid to have fun.

By the way, I don't blame you for daydreaming about the nights when you and your lover will go to bed together in the nest of the home God gives you. The couple in Solomon's Song of Songs did. In fact, I think it would be fitting to close with the poetry of that often-ignored book:

> I belong to my lover,
>   and his desire is for me.
> Come, my lover, let us go to the countryside,

let us spend the night in the villages.
Let us go early to the vineyards
   to see if the vines have budded,
   if their blossoms have opened,
   and if the pomegranates are in bloom—
   there I will give you my love.
The mandrakes send out their fragrance,
   and at our door is every delicacy,
both new and old,
   that I have stored up for you, my lover.

Song of Songs 7:10–13

2️⃣0️⃣ **Purity**

Found in the Attic

*To the pure, all things are pure, but to those who are corrupted
and do not believe, nothing is pure. In fact, both their minds and
consciences are corrupted* (Titus 1:15).

A Sunday-school teacher was quizzing her class on an
old proverb she had taught them the week before; "Now, cleanliness is next to what?"

One of the boys in the back piped up, "Impossible."

Just as staying physically clean is a struggle for dirt-loving kids,
moral cleanness has fallen on hard times with adults. Purity is something stashed in the attic with Granny's long bloomers. Today that
stuff is unfashionable. Mention virginity and right away people
snicker. Goodie-goodie is out; casual sex is in. People who wait until
marriage to "do it" are slandered, ridiculed, and made out to be
dumbbells. It reminds me of a Scripture verse which has been
tucked away in the same attic trunk with Granny's outdated clothes:

> Woe to those who call evil good
>   and good evil,
> who put darkness for light
>   and light for darkness,

who put bitter for sweet
and sweet for bitter.

Isa. 5:20

That sounds like something I call "the numbing effect." When you beat a person with a club long enough, he gets to where he can't feel it anymore. But the real damage has just begun. That's what happened to purity. It got bombarded so much with sex-talk that it grew numb. Changes gradually crept in. No one was wise to how very terrible things were getting, because they were dazed by the so-called sexual revolution.

Homosexuality is one example. Radio psychologists, newspaper advice columnists, and even "ministers," have told us to accept the gays. They say nothing is abnormal about that lifestyle. At first we hollered back that they were full of bunk—queers are queers! But after gay-rights supporters finished bull-whipping us with the disgusting "thrills" of loving someone of the same sex, there was nothing left to shock us. Why blush now? Every impure detail has been told and retold. Still, truth is truth: gays are not *gay*. Homosexual acts are sick and sinful. But this last paragraph, if printed in tomorrow's newspaper, would raise enough stink to start rioting in the "homo" community and protests from their sympathizers. What's worse: more than half of the people who read it would only laugh. That's the power of "the numbing effect."

Frankly, that scares me. Why? Because calluses don't wear off easily. If we learn to take sexual impurity of all kinds right in stride, will real purity have a chance of surviving?

Let's dig purity out of the attic, scrape off the cobwebs, and give it a little mouth-to-mouth resuscitation. Look it over and give me your opinion. Can it live in our society?

Purity means sexual balance. It doesn't mean we have to be a bunch of prudes. We don't have to jam our heads into the sand like ostriches, hushing all sex-talk. But purity does put handcuffs on immodesty and immorality. Sensible censorship is a necessity. And, for purity to stay pure, it cannot change. In other words, what God's Word calls "impure" must always be considered impure.

Purity means being "straight." By that I mean that sex stays inside the relationship it was created for—marriage. No matter how loudly the uncivilized alley cats want to scream, cleanliness refuses to grow calluses. It hangs with the words of 1 Thessalonians 4:3–5, 7:

> It is God's will that you should be holy; that you should avoid sexual immorality; that each of you should learn to control his own body in a way that is holy and honorable, not in passionate lust like the heathen, who do not know God. . . . For God did not call us to be impure, but to live a holy life.

Purity means blameless living. I didn't say "faultless" living. All of us have faults. Blamelessness means no one can accuse you; they can't point a finger and say, "Ah-ah!"

Let me illustrate. After his mother had been in the hospital for a long time, a little boy decided to cheer her up with a homemade card. He drew a rather messy picture of "Mommy," using wrong colors in wrong places. Inside of it he wrote:

Dir Mommie,
Are you evir going to come home? I missd you verry much plese git well soon. We cant go on forevir, you no.

Love Bobby

The card wasn't exactly "faultless"; it was full of mistakes. But it *was* "blameless." The pure love is plain to see. Get the idea? A blameless life is a pure life.

Now back to the question: Can purity live in our society? You answer it for yourself. And please don't say, "Impossible!" Because purity is counting on your help.

Visit the attic and go back to the future.

21 Divorce

Gone with the Wind

[*Jesus said:*] *"So, they are no longer two, but one. Therefore, what God has joined together, let man not separate"* (Matt. 19:6).

Chuck Swindoll relates a cute story in his book, *Strike the Original Match*. I love it. A four-year-old named Suzie was bubbling with excitement upon returning home from nursery school. She had just heard the tale of Snow White for the first time and couldn't wait to tell her mommy. With vivid color she retold each detail. After describing how Prince Charming came riding up on his white charger to kiss Snow White back to life, Suzie then asked: "And, Mommy, do you know what happened next?"

"Yes," her mother answered, "they lived happily ever after."

"No," Suzie said with disappointment, ". . . they got married."

These days one is not necessarily the same as the other. In fact, if a postscript were added to Snow White's story, it might say:

A few years later Snow and Charming starting arguing. The good prince went to spending a lot of time at the corner pub. One night, instead of returning to the palace, he went home with one of the barmaids. Snow suspected him, and after some clever detective work she caught him in bed with the other woman. When Charming came home, he found his bags packed and waiting on the palace drawbridge. The next day Snow filed for divorce in district court.

Why put a chapter about divorce in a book to graduates? Well, I figure at least a few of you will eventually get married. With the general order for modern-day romance being dating, marriage, divorce, remarriage, I thought it would be a good idea to chat about it now. *Before* you have a chance to wade in over your head. Maybe it will save you from ending up a dreary statistic.

No, I'm not trying to talk you out of getting married, if that's part of your immediate plans. It's not my place to interfere with your future. That's *your* business, but helping couples stay together is mine.

Perhaps "tying the knot" isn't on the front burner for you, but you do expect to be hitched someday. That, too, is fine. Don't feel like a baby because your immediate plans don't include life's most serious step. Your time will come.

The things I want to pass along will be relevant, whenever your wedding bells start to ring. This year or ten years from now, these timeless reminders can help ward off a ton of regret.

Be sure. I know, I know—everybody says that. But one more time won't hurt. Once it's done, it's done. Divorce has become popular largely because couples rush in, find out they actually had nothing in common, and so decide to split. Can you truly open up to your dream lover? Is he or she your friend, too? Are your personalities compatible? How much do you really know about him or her? Are you convinced that this is God's choice for you? Mull these questions over when Cupid nails you.

You see, if you start hating this person after marriage (of course, nobody ever expects that to happen), you will quite likely be tempted to violate the Virtue Commandment. Don't just be blissful when entering marriage; be realistic.

Work at it. This is something no prospective husband or bride thinks about. Really! Most people have a fairy-tale haze over their brains, figuring they'll live happily ever after. It doesn't happen that way. Sorry to burst your bubble, but that jazz is true only in romance novels. If you see a good marriage, it's because both partners have worked hard and are still working to make it that way.

After the honeymoon, the task begins. And it gets tough sometimes. To make it worse, Satan knows exactly when to bring along some alluring gal or tender, caring man to tempt you to blow the whole relationship. If you've made up your mind to work, you can keep your record clean on the seventh commandment.

Divorce is no solution. Oh, it may look like the best way out. But few people find it satisfying. And in over 66 percent of the cases of those who remarry, the second partner is a carbon copy of the first. And often worse! Which means the divorce solved nothing.

Yearning to get out of a marriage—hoping to remarry someday and be happy again—is ignorance of God's reason for The Virtue Commandment. A happy home is not something we stumble upon by accident. Nor is it something that comes through multiple attempts. No, we get it the old-fashioned way—we earn it! How? By piecing together each principle of the Ten Commandments within the family boundaries. These principles—not divorce—are your solution.

You may have been skipping over this chapter, thinking it doesn't pertain to you and never will. I wish you'd read it once every six months, whether you're engaged or not. Because I think we can put a stop to the divorce-remarriage cycle by conditioning individuals before they become couples.

Storybook endings take a lifetime to write.

PART 8

The Samaritan Commandment

"You shall not steal" (Exod. 20:15).

22 Greed

Leave Home Without It

For of this you can be sure: No immoral, impure or greedy person—such a man is an idolater—has any inheritance in the kingdom of Christ and of God (Eph. 5:5).

You know the credit-card slogan that goes: "American Express—Don't leave home without it"? Well, flip-flop that for greediness: "Leave home without it!"

Somebody needs to pass along that advice to professional athletes. The Major League Baseball Players Association recently finished Strike III. I waited with anticipation for an umpire to yell, "Yer out!" Even with the national pastime the cry is no longer "Play ball!" No, the howl is the same one we hear everywhere else: "More money!" I think the average American has a hard time relating to multi-year, million-dollar contracts. Most of us won't earn that much in a lifetime.

But let's not single out athletes. Tell me of one psychiatrist who is really worth $100 an hour. And answer whether $200 sounds like a reasonable fee for a simple forty-five minute medical consultation. What corporate executive—regardless of personal charisma—is truly worth the megabucks he or she earns? Listen, I'm not condemning people for making big money. I want to get across a different point, that prosperity in America is turning us into money hogs!

103

Not all psychiatrists, doctors, executives, and so on, are slobbering after dollars like a drunk for cheap wine. No doubt most of them work very hard for their income. I'm talking about a fever that has fallen on our country like acid rain—the passion for more, more, more! And feeling convinced that we *deserve* it—that if we don't get it, we've been robbed, gyped, cheated, ripped-off. Striking, complaining, picketing, if we don't get our hunk of the pie. Is this part of the American Way? Baloney!

Okay, so inflation is going bonkers, and bigger salaries don't necessarily mean greater income. It takes more to feed a family these days. Buying a house costs an arm and a leg. College tuition is murder. Car payments are ridiculous. Take-home pay shrinks, and the national debt makes matters worse. All right, already!

We interrupt this argument to bring you some special questions. When E. F. Hutton speaks, do you listen? Do you even know who E. F. Hutton is? How about Merrill Lynch? Ever hear of Wall Street? You know, the place where the Great Depression started. Yeah, the street where greedy brokers jumped out of tall buildings when they went broke back in 1929. We didn't learn much from it, did we?

Stop. Take a deep breath. Is your head spinning yet? Say "Hello!" to the real world. Up to now you've probably been happy to make a minimum wage or slightly better. Having enough money left over to buy some french fries is enough for you. And here I've been rambling on about the world of money. Forgive me. I did it to illustrate how naive some of you are to the Greed Creed. It goes like this: "I promise to break my fool neck to get every penny that's coming to me. I will work ninety-hour weeks. I will sacrifice my family. I will not allow God to get in my way. I promise to become a self-made millionaire, even if it kills me."

Nobody says it aloud. There's no lodge meeting where all the money-mongers raise a toast. The Greed Creed is sort of a silent agreement that people vow to themselves. They may not use those very words; often it is just a decision, a long-term goal. However, they live the creed as if they had said it.

So why tell you? Because it's usually in these first few years after graduation that Mother Greed starts to wrap her loving arms around her victims. Being a Christian does not give you automatic protection. The time to start thinking about the role of the green-back in your life is now.

Timothy was young when Paul talked bank accounts with him. His money-wise advice is still good today:

> But godliness with contentment is great gain. For we brought nothing into the world, and we can take nothing out of it. But if we have food and clothing, we will be content with that. People who want to get rich fall into temptation and a trap and into many foolish and harmful desires that plunge men into ruin and destruction. For the love of money is a root of all kinds of evil. Some people, eager for money, have wandered from the faith and pierced themselves with many griefs (1 Tim. 6:6–10).

I once heard an old saying that makes a fine replacement for the Greed Creed. It goes like this: "Make the very most of all you've got and make the very least of what you can't get yet!" Isn't that a dandy? Or as another wise sage said, "The best way to live happily ever after is not to be after too much."

Jesus said it this way, "What good is it for a man to gain the whole world, yet forfeit his soul?" (Mark 8:36).

Greediness is an incredible lust. Few emotions can send our fever so high. Mention that "thar's gold in them thar hills" and everybody grabs a pick and shovel. Our sin nature digs that stuff. It caused Mark Twain to remark: "Such is the human race. Often it does seem a pity that Noah and his party didn't miss the boat."

How does this relate to "You shall not steal"? Think about it. What inspires a thief to heist a haul of goods? Greed. Right? Even us honest folk need help with that emotion.

Let me close this off with an anonymous tidbit about the seven ages of man:

First age: A child sees the earth.

Second age: He wants it.

Third age: He hustles to get it.

Fourth age: He decides to be satisfied with about half of it.

Fifth age: He would be satisfied with less than half of it.

| Sixth age: | He is now content to possess a two-by-six-foot section of it. |
| Seventh age: | He gets it. |

Thank God, we won't need money in the beyond.

23 Selfishness

The Fast-Food Philosophy

Their destiny is destruction, their god is their stomach, and their glory is in their shame. Their mind is on earthly things (Phil. 3:19).

Fast-food franchises cater to our hustle-bustle schedules. When they slap our midday manna on a tray, they accommodate our every need. The fifteen-minute eatery is the product of a society on the move. It also reflects today's underlying approach to life: "Serve me, serve me quickly, and clean up after me."

Stealing. It comes in more flavors than burglary, embezzlement, and shoplifting. That's what Jesus was trying to say when he told the parable of the good Samaritan. You can read the incident in Luke 10:25–37.

As the story goes, Mr. Joe Unlucky was on his way home from the supermarket when a bunch of hoodlums mugged him. The thugs beat him up, stripped him, and swiped his loot. Then they kicked him over into a ditch, leaving him half-dead. Sounds like New York City, huh? Obviously, they broke the eighth commandment.

While Joe lay in the ditch praying for an ambulance to come, a priest came walking by. Praise God! Religious people are always loving helpers of mankind. Right? Wrong. When Father I'm-Too-

Good saw the poor sap, he crossed at the intersection and passed by on the opposite side of the street.

Problem: I know he didn't actually steal anything, but was he true to the spirit of the eighth commandment?

Later that afternoon, a Levite came by. A Levite was higher up on the totem pole than a plain priest. So what did Bishop I'm-Too-Busy do when he saw Joe? The same song and dance as his underling. He crossed at the intersection and went over to the ice-cream parlor to have a chocolate malt. And though he didn't steal anything either, I can't shake the feeling that he, too, was almost as guilty as the guys who did.

Finally a Samaritan came by. (In a Jew's eye, a Samaritan was equivalent to a cross between a lamb and a pig; Samaritans were half-Hebrew, half-Gentile. Since Jesus was telling the story to a Jewish lawyer, you can be sure the Samaritan bit didn't set well.) The Samaritan came through for ol' Joe. He bandaged him up, gave him taxi service on a donkey to a nearby inn, and paid for Joe's room for as long as he needed it. He even promised to come back to check on Joe and pay any extra expenses that came up. Talk about unselfishness! I believe that's part of what God had in mind when he composed the "you shall not steal" commandment.

Whether or not you agree with me, those two "religious" passersby were no nicer than the scoundrels who did the actual robbing. All of them were guilty of selfishness of one kind or another. One group took from Joe; the others refused to give to him. In this case the difference is hard to measure.

Are you beginning to see that the Ten Commandments were not merely intended to be sharp one-liners or the most-often-quoted readings from God's Mount Sinai show? When we break down each individual commandment, they cover a lot of territory. Don't they turn out to be much more than a list of "do's and don'ts"?

As I've been writing this, I've been listening to the beautiful strains of Tchaikovsky's *Swan Lake* and *Sleeping Beauty*. It has reminded me of something said by Leonard Bernstein, the famous composer and conductor, when asked which musical instrument is the most difficult to play. His comeback was terrific: "Second fiddle. I can get plenty of first violinists, but to find one who plays *second* violin with as much enthusiasm or *second* French horn or *second* flute, now that's a problem. And yet if no one plays second, we have no harmony."

We are conditioned to want to be first at everything and to have the best portion. Is that bad? Not necessarily. In my book *You're Worth It!* I harp on the importance of having self-confidence and a winner's outlook. But we should not want first regardless of cost. Putting self that highly is bound to cause conflict, and pity anyone like the poor beaten victim who gets in our way! If all we're interested in is squeezing every drop out of life that we can get, then we'll certainly pass him by. A few might even be tempted to join the crooks who jumped him to begin with.

You must learn this quickly: self is a thief. It steals the real values from life. Self wants to be served immediately and cleaned up after. It wants its choices regardless of the pain to others. Self can be downright criminal if we let it.

> Lord Crucified, O mark Thy holy Cross
> On motive, preference, all fond desires,
> On that which self in any form inspires
> Set Thou that sign of loss.
>
> And when the touch of death is here and there
> Laid on a thing most precious in our eyes,
> Let us not wonder, let us recognize
> The answer to this prayer.
>
> Amy Carmichael

Selfishness has been called "the sin that bleeds." As a black-mailer leeches off his prey, selfishness bleeds life of fairness and mercy. Just as a kidnapper drains his pigeon, selfishness takes for ransom the blessings of others. And as a con artist stings his mark, selfishness sucks the meaning out of humble integrity. A self-filled person, though he never steals a thing, can leave people with the feeling that they have been taken.

Enjoy your next burger 'n fries, but use that time to chew on this, too. Call it "food for thought."

24 Giving

Sweet Release

For where your treasure is, there your heart will be also (Matt. 6:21).

The New Hebrides Islands are just west of Fiji and Samoa in the South Pacific. Farther west is the Coral Sea. Southwest is Australia. And you thought World Geography was over!

Anyway, one of the old heathen customs in New Hebrides calls for a sacrifice of pigs. The "sacred men" roast a hog and cut off the pig's tail, presenting it to the gods as their fair share of the feast. The worshipers eat what's left. Of course, their silly gods don't exist. But pigs' tails, indeed! How chintzy can you get? It reminds me of the way too many Christians act when they give to the True God.

George Muller, a prayer warrior from the nineteenth century, once said, "God measures what we give by what we keep." Good insight. The heathens in New Hebrides keep plenty. I wonder how much most Christians give in comparison to what they keep?

Where does this fit in with the commandment that forbids stealing? Look up Malachi 3:8–10. God is giving Israel a good talking-to in the passage. However, the application for us is plain to see:

> "Will a man rob God? Yet you rob me.
>
> "But you ask, 'How do we rob you?'
>
> "In tithes and offerings. You are under a curse—the whole nation of you—because you are robbing me. Bring the whole tithe into the storehouse, that there may be food in my house. Test me in this," says the LORD Almighty, "and see if I will not throw open the floodgates of heaven and pour out so much blessing that you will not have room enough for it."

Robbing God. Doesn't that qualify for violating the eighth commandment? Sure it does. Anyone who has trusted Jesus Christ should feel a sense of debt. Those who try to wriggle out of it are cheapskates. Don't misunderstand. We can't buy what Jesus Christ has to offer. Eternal life is a gift, and we could never give enough in a million years to repay what he did by dying for our sins. Yet we do owe him—a lot more than 10 percent of our money. Since he died in our place, we owe him everything. Everything? Yes, everything: money, possessions, family, talents, and ourselves.

That brings me to Mark 12:41–44. Great story. Jesus had just finished a horrible day of debate with the legalistic Pharisees, the grueling Herodians, the earthly minded Sadducees, and the nitpicking scribes. The Lord was dog-tired. Wishing to get a break from the troublemakers, he sat down in the temple courts opposite the place where the offerings were put.

The contribution boxes in those days were called "trumpets," because of their trumpetlike shape. And get this: people would slam their money into the trumpets to make a loud racket. The bigger the coin, the better the noise and the greater the attention. Now you know why the word *trumpets* was appropriate. They were a glorified means of "tooting your own horn."

Jesus rested while the show-offs "trumpeted" their offerings. No doubt he grew bored with the clatter and clangs, wondering if anybody knew the meaning of sacrifice. Suddenly, another sound! A quiet sound. The trumpet was barely speaking, but it was blowing a beautiful song. A poor widow had humbly dropped in two mites. The coin she gave was known as a *lepton,* meaning "thin one." The *lepton* was the tiniest coin, and it was equal to one-sixteenth of a cent. So the widow didn't even put in her two-cents' worth.

But the trumpet's tinkle was sweet music to Jesus' ears. He yelled for his disciples to come see the widow. And as she walked away he taught them: "There, my friends, is a lady who knows more about giving than the rest of the crowd that's gone by. Oh, yeah, they threw in their fat, noisy coins. But they gave only what they could afford. She gave her all" (*see* Mark 6:43–44). The pagans at New Hebrides might say, "She went *whole* hog!"

Was Jesus trying to say that we should put everything we have in the offering plate? No. But we should acknowledge that all we have is God's, and then do our best to use it for his glory. After all, God *is* the rightful owner.

The widow's gift was not really a gift of money. One-eighth of a penny wouldn't have made a dent in the temple's light bill. Her offering was a gift of self. Those two mites were a mere symbol that she had already given back to God the richest thing she owned—herself! Shame on us for thinking at times that we can buy God off with our money. All along, we keep back ourselves. That, too, is stealing. (Ouch! These commandments cut to the heart!)

I came upon some verses by my favorite poet the other day. He writes all the best stuff. His name is spread far and abroad. Another reason I like him is that his name alone tells us how we ought to go about our giving.

> One by one He took them from me
>   All the things I valued most;
> 'Til I was empty-handed,
>   Every glittering toy was lost.
> And I walked earth's highways, grieving,
>   In my rags and poverty.
> Until I heard His voice inviting,
>   "Lift those empty hands to Me!"
>
> Then I turned my hands toward heaven,
>   And He filled them with a store
> Of His own transcendent riches,
>   'Til they could contain no more.
> And at last I comprehended
>   With my stupid mind, and dull,
> That God cannot pour His riches
>   Into hands already full.
>
>> Signed,
>> Anonymous

"Anonymous" and the widow have a tremendous trait in common: neither likes to blow his or her own trumpet. But they're not "pigtail Christians" either. If you know what I mean.

PART **9**

The Genuineness Commandment

"You shall not give false testimony against your neighbor" (Exod. 20:16).

25 Transparency

See-Through Living

Rather, we have renounced secret and shameful ways; we do not use deception, nor do we distort the word of God. On the contrary, by setting forth the truth plainly we commend ourselves to every man's conscience in the sight of God (2 Cor. 4:2).

The kiss of Judas. Never in history has there been a greater deception; never has fakery worn such a vile mask. Chapter 26 of Matthew follows the trail of his dirty deed. Let's recreate the scene. And I want you, as much as possible, to imagine you are there.

Many Bible scholars believe that Judas was a member of an underground, revolutionary, political group. As a secret agent, he was never truly interested in the spiritual teachings of Christ. Judas wanted the government overthrown. Jesus was the perfect guy to lead the revolution, he thought. But Jesus was a slowpoke; he wouldn't hurry up and do what Judas assumed he had come to do—start a new kingdom. Actually the Lord did start a new kingdom, but it was spiritual, not political.

Confused? Hang in there. When Judas realized that Jesus was not a political activist, he tried to think of a way to force him to begin the rebellion. This was a complete secret, for Judas had kept it hidden from everyone. Thus, his decision:

> Then one of the Twelve—the one called Judas Iscariot—went to the chief priests and asked, "What are you willing to give me if I hand him over to you?" So they counted out for him thirty silver coins. From then on Judas watched for an opportunity to hand him over (Matt. 26:14–16).

Judas figured that Jesus would have to use his power to escape the chief priests, and then the revolution could begin. So, not only was he betraying Jesus, but he was also using him. Judas didn't have a godly bone in his body; he was totally blind to the real reason why Christ had come.

Whether or not this view is accurate, one thing is for certain: Judas was a shadowy person. No one knew the real him (except Jesus). Evidently none of the disciples suspected he was a liar, a cheat, and a betrayer. Because, when Jesus said that one of them was up to no good, they all replied, "Surely not I, Lord?" (Matt. 26:22). They never dreamed the scoundrel was Judas. He had done a fine job of fooling them all.

Later that night Judas started showing his true colors. By dawn he had led a mob up to Gethsemane. Sit down on one of the large garden rocks and listen in:

> While he [Jesus] was still speaking, Judas, one of the Twelve, arrived. With him was a large crowd armed with swords and clubs, sent from the chief priests and the elders of the people. Now the betrayer had arranged a signal with them: "The one I kiss is the man; arrest him." Going at once to Jesus, Judas said, "Greetings, Rabbi!" and kissed him (Matt. 26:47–49).

Crash! The Genuineness Commandment was broken into a trillion smithereens by Judas. His make-believe kindness makes me want to vomit. Did you hear his sugary tone? "Greetings, Rabbi!" Yuk!

Jesus wasn't fooled. He looked Judas square in the eye and said, "Friend, do what you came for" (v. 50). Pow! I bet that punch took the traitor by surprise. I can just see the cocky smirk melting and dripping off his face. Jesus knew the truth about him.

Bulletin: Jesus knows the truth about each of us, too. Furthermore, he wants us to cut out playing hide and seek. Jesus wants us to be ourselves. No cheap imitations. No trickery. No betrayal. No big secrets. Jesus wants transparency.

We are to be windows, not doors. Instead of closing people out, we should let them see in—to Christ. We should be sheer, not shadowy. But how? By leaving the shades up. Lest we become known as "shady" people.

Openness. If you are in Gethsemane with Jesus, you have nothing to be ashamed of. The Judases, who are filled with deception, are the ones who must keep their curtains down. If you're not trying to decoy people, then why pretend to be something you're not? It all comes out eventually.

Why not be yourself? Turn loose of your fears of failure and rejection. Stop acting and stop trying to be perfect. Say to the world, "This is me! Take me or leave me." Whether they take you or not doesn't really matter, because Jesus does. Yet the world usually accepts those with enough confidence to be themselves. But it hates a phony.

Motives. If Judas was a member of a radical group, his motives for following Christ were also deceitful. Motives—what makes people do what they do—are very much a part of being transparent. Those driven by flimsy ambition must keep their whimsy a secret. They can't risk someone's discovering the real reason behind what they do.

A clear conscience and a pure heart are the best medicine for right motivation. Otherwise one must build lie upon lie to keep the truth from being known. However, if the truth about you is clean-spirited, it needs no veneer.

Simplicity. A basic plan for living keeps life understandable. But the more complicated a person allows himself to get, the more opaque he becomes. A simple goal—such as "Do it all for the glory of God" (1 Cor. 10:31)—can prevent you from becoming muddy and blurry and misunderstood.

Judas was too complex. He had to be too many people, had to

wear too many masks. When he realized this, it was too late. And he hated himself—although, after studying him, I believe he would have done it again, given the chance, because he never allowed himself to be transparent before Christ; he was always hiding out.

Even his kiss was a cover-up.

26 Ethics

Strategy for Sticky Situations

> *We demolish arguments and every pretension that sets itself up against the knowledge of God, and we take captive every thought to make it obedient to Christ* (2 Cor. 10:5).

What is an "ethic"? It sounds like some kind of insect. Or is it a bird? Maybe it's a disease, like measles, except that it produces spots only in your armpits. Then again, could it be the name of a foreign sports car? Ah! I've got it: an "ethic" is a special type of Eskimo bobsled.

All wrong, but of course you knew that. However, the world is getting awfully short on ethics these days. Noah Webster—the guy who thought in alphabetical order—defined it as "a principle of conduct." *Ethics* are the things that influence us to make choices between right and wrong, bad and worse, or good and best. One's ethics should be based on *truth*.

Let me give you some sticky situations in which a person must make an ethical decision. In all of these circumstances, morality plays a part. Society will argue for years about which choice is right. The principles of God's Word are also on the line. What do you believe is the ethical thing to do in these problem cases?

"Can premarital sex and living together help a couple decide if they are compatible? After all, why should we risk divorce if it is possible that we don't blend well?"

"Sixteen is too young for a girl to be a mother. We know she could give the baby up for adoption, but we don't want her to go through the ordeal by carrying a child and giving birth. Is an abortion that bad an idea?"

"Surely one drink can't hurt anybody. I don't advocate drunkenness, but a casual, social drink has to be okay. Right?"

"The old man's practically dead anyway. Why go to all the trouble of keeping him alive on these machines when he will probably die tomorrow. Why not pull the plug?"

"Mixing some races is okay, but come on . . . Blacks and Whites?"

"Marijuana isn't that much different from alcohol. Why shouldn't it be legalized? For that matter, why not legalize prostitution, too? Both products could help raise tax revenues if they became legitimate businesses."

Your ethics will determine your choices. Basically there are two lines of thinking: Christian ethics and situation ethics. The difference? The first is based upon scriptural principles; the second is based upon what the *individual* feels is best. A framework of Christian ethics has no pat answers, but it does have some definite wisdom. With God's system there's no guarantee that all things will come out as you had planned, but at least you can have the peace of knowing you are seeking his will.

Situation ethics? Well, that's hard to describe. This code has no code. It's a cousin to the do-your-own-thing mentality. People are free to figure out things for themselves. Choices aren't based upon a clear-cut true or false, but upon circumstances and emotions. There are no rules or authorities, only personal insight. Situation-ethics lovers hate commandments. They reject anything that prevents them from being able to fool themselves. There is nothing genuine about this creed; it's a pack of lies.

In any sticky situation, Christian ethics point the route to go. Here's how it works. Ask yourself the following questions and pray. God will impress upon your heart the direction in which to head.

1. *Which choice will build a stronger relationship with Jesus*

Christ in my life? Jesus said, "Whoever has my commands and obeys them, he is the one who loves me . . ." (John 14:21). You can't get closer to Christ by doing it *your* way.

2. *Does the Bible have anything to say?* Humanists (the champions of the situation-ethics cause) scream when they hear this. To them, morality is a party-pooper. It just isn't fair. Why do they get so riled over spiritual input? I guess they don't like truth.

3. *What is fair and honorable?* Some people have no ethics. Like cheaters, liars, and con artists. Part of the Christian way is justice. Jesus was fair and taught that we should be fair, too. He laid out a straightforward plan: "Simply let your 'Yes' be 'Yes,' and your 'No,' 'No'; anything beyond this comes from the evil one" (Matt. 5:37).

4. *What am I responsible for?* If you have an obligation in the situation, you must face yourself—conscience and all—and agree to fulfill it. Duty has become a questionable four-letter word in our age. Still, having ethics calls for a decent person to be responsible. A denial of duty is quite like a lie.

5. *What will strengthen my testimony for Christ?* A choice that makes you two-faced is worthless. If you opt for the dark alley over the broad lighted street, you will ruin every principle you stand for.

To have an ethical stance takes courage; it got Daniel a room in the lions' hotel. A code of ethics requires consistency; Elisha was straight as an arrow. Ethics can be expensive; almost every disciple was martyred. Ethical living demands character; that is why the original code was given to Moses.

God carved the Christian ethic into stone. Jesus goes a step further—he carves it into our hearts through grace.

27 Defection

The AWOL Syndrome

[F]or Demas, because he loved this world, has deserted me and has gone to Thessalonica . . . (2 Tim. 4:10).

Absent WithOut Leave" is the military's name for it. But it goes by a number of other different titles as well: dropout, quitter, runaway, over the wall, burnout.

One who defects does not remain *true*. And that is what the spirit of the genuine Commandment is all about—being a true witness of Jesus Christ. Yes, I know that the primary warning of the ninth commandment was against lying. But the functional handle to grab is: "Live a genuine life." When a Christian goes AWOL, it is like admitting that his or her life was a big lie.

There are various levels of going AWOL from the army of God. All of them are serious, but some are more drastic than others. Many fugitives come back to a fruitful ministry of serving Christ. Others become prisoners of the enemy—Satan—and never make it back.

Let's look at four AWOL cases in the Bible. They are arranged in order, with the first one being "urgent" and the last one being "no joke!"

AWOL Case #1: If you were to read Acts 13:13, you might not notice a problem. It says that "John left them to return to Jerusalem." Who would dream that he had quitting on his mind? The "John" in this passage was John Mark, cousin of Barnabas (Col. 4:10). At the time of this little voyage, he was a young man. My guess is that he cut out because he was scared to death.

How do we know that he dropped out? Because, when Paul and Barnabas got ready to go on the second voyage, ol' Barney wanted to bring along John Mark again. Paul would not hear of it: "Barnabas wanted to take John, also called Mark, with them, but Paul did not think it wise to take him, because he had *deserted* them in Pamphylia and *had not continued with them in the work*" (Acts 15:37–38, italics added).

If John Mark was scared, I don't blame him. Being a foreign missionary is a tough job. Thank God for Barnabas! He split from Paul, rescued his cousin, and together they went on to Cyprus. As a result we have a gospel account written by Mark. Even Paul came to value him: ". . . Get Mark and bring him with you, because he is helpful to me in my ministry" (2 Tim. 4:11). You see, AWOL doesn't have to become permanent out-and-out defection.

AWOL Case #2: In 1 Kings 19:3 we find Elijah running like a rabbit from Jezebel. He stopped under a broom tree to whine and cry before really going over the hill to Mount Horeb. His disappearing act was a forty-day jaunt. God called to Elijah in a gentle whisper (v. 12), but the frightened prophet was reluctant to go back and face the fierce queen.

Eventually Elijah did go back, but his effectiveness was weakened. So he was instructed to train a replacement. Soon Elisha came off the bench to take Elijah's place. And though we remember Elijah with honor, his spell of chicken-heartedness remains a black spot on his record.

AWOL Case #3: Jonah. Who else? You know the story so well that you don't need to look it up. God told him to go one way, and he went the other. However, his Caribbean cruise turned into a nightmare vacation. He got thrown overboard! And then he became whale bait! What a rotten way to spend three days and three nights on the open seas.

Jonah did his duty when the whale spit him out. Nineveh—the Las Vegas of that day—repented when its people heard his message. All was quiet on the Eastern Front. Except for Jonah! He went into despair because he had wanted Nineveh wiped out. Some guy, huh? As far as we know, this burnout became the end of his ministry. AWOL was a part of Jonah's character, and it's like that with a lot of people.

AWOL Case #4: In the other three cases there was at least some salvage operation, if not complete recovery. Not with Demas. Once he went over the wall, he never came back. Total defection. The verse that heads this chapter tells us why he deserted: "because he loved this world." Some people quit because they don't want to give up an evil lifestyle.

Maybe you've been thinking about going AWOL. The Christian life has been no picnic, and temptation looks so inviting. In the back of your mind you may be wondering if it would make any difference if you went over the wall. "Would anyone even notice?" you ask yourself. "Would anyone care?" You feel surrounded. "Why not forget this Christianity business?"

In World War I a commanding general—ordered to "Defend the position to death!"—flashed the following battle report:

Bombardment began at midnight.

  2:30 A.M. Bombing is worse on the right.

  4:15 A.M. We have stood strong, but are now surrounded on our right.

  7:45 A.M. The right has fallen.

  10:11 A.M. Holding our position.

  11:45 A.M. Enemy overrunning us. Trying to hold.

  12:05 P.M. Done for!

I'm sure the general, as well as his men, must have considered going AWOL from the battle. But from deep within something prevented them: they were *true* and *faithful*. They persevered.

But Demas went to Thessalonica.

PART

10

The Contentment Commandment

"You shall not covet your neighbor's house. You shall not covet your neighbor's wife, or his manservant or maidservant, his ox or donkey, or anything that belongs to your neighbor" (Exod. 20:17).

28 Materialism

Comfortable Christianity

*They were stoned; they were sawed in two; they were put to death by the sword. They went about in sheepskins and goatskins, destitute, persecuted and mistreated—**the world was not worthy of them** ... (Heb. 11:37–38, emphasis added).*

After telling the story of the rich man and Lazarus to his Sunday-school class, the teacher then asked, "Now, boys, which would you rather be—the rich man or Lazarus?"

A sharp-witted boy replied: "I'd want to be the rich man while I'm living and Lazarus when I die."

He said a mouthful. The general public thinks the same way. If it comes down to a choice between being comfortable or being committed, many would choose to be like the rich man. However, in the hereafter they hope to be like Lazarus. (Need the background to this story? Try Luke 16:19–31).

"Can a person have both?" you ask. The answer is that it really depends upon the person. The track record of humanity on materialism reads like the report on a losing horse at Churchill Downs: pretty disappointing. Very few of us are able to handle a life of ease without falling plum asleep. The love of "things" even drives some people to an early grave.

127

In a cemetery in England a tombstone bears this inscription: SHE DIED FOR WANT OF THINGS. Alongside that marker stands another, which reads: HE DIED TRYING TO GIVE THEM TO HER.

Maybe you know a couple just like that. She can't get enough, and he can't keep up with the rate at which she writes checks. Recently I heard of a humdinger like this. The husband was working like a madman and making good money. In fact, he was probably too preoccupied with how much he earned. His wife was buying quite a bit of stuff, but he wasn't paying much attention.

Then the bottom dropped out. He began getting some strange mail. First came a repossession notice on his truck and then one on his boat. Next came a letter from the bank, warning him that he had missed three house payments and they were ready to evict him. His three major-credit-card corporations wrote that he was over his limit. Since he rarely went on buying sprees and always sent his payments on time, all this came as a shock.

Come to find out, his wife had been retrieving the payments from the mailbox before the mailman came by. Then there would be enough checking-account money for the items she wanted. By screening out warning notices in the mail, she was able to keep this secret until she finally got careless. The credit-card mix-up was also her handiwork. The husband was so berserk, I thought he was going to have a coronary. The two tombstones in England would fit nicely on their graves, don't you think?

Admit it. You've got a strong urge for some luxury. It is with embarrassment that I confess mine: a Mercedes 450 SL. Go ahead and laugh. Point your finger at me and ridicule me; I deserve it. But I'm not going to break the ninth commandment and lie to you.

I want a red one. Black interior. Dashboard like an airplane cockpit. Sun-roof. Hi-fidelity stereo with cassette deck and compact disc player. Five-speed, but I'd settle for an automatic. Electric everything, including automatic seat-warmers. The whole nine yards.

You're right, that's materialistic. And covetous. Many times the Lord has told me to get my heart straight. And I've improved at my "gimme" binges. Now I only go nuts when I *see* a Mercedes. I used to go nuts when I heard the name.

That's a luxury item, which means something we don't really

need, but we think we'd be a lot happier if we got it. Don't play holier-than-thou with me: you've got such a yen, too. Maybe it's for a well-situated home in the mountains . . . or a huge, handwoven Oriental rug . . . or a new wardrobe . . . or a houseful of the finest furnishings . . . or a speedboat . . . or the highest-quality stereo equipment money can buy . . . or a back-yard swimming pool . . . or a flashy golf cart and a $700 set of clubs . . . or an original painting by Rembrandt. So stop acting like you never covet.

Personally I don't think wishing is wrong. But when wishing becomes craving, and craving becomes "I can't live without it," then something is off-base. Material possessions in themselves are not sinful. Job, Abraham, David, and Solomon had great wealth. And, except for Solomon in his later years, they kept a pretty good perspective on their holdings.

When it comes to the Contentment Commandment, the greatest New Testament principle to remember is: "There is a love that God hates."

> Do not love the world or anything in the world. If anyone loves the world, the love of the Father is not in him. For everything in the world—the cravings of sinful man, the lust of his eyes and the boasting of what he has and does—comes not from the Father but from the world. The world and its desires pass away, but the man who does the will of God lives forever (1 John 2:15–17).

The verses that introduce this chapter are part of the postscript to chapter 11 of Hebrews, the Faith Hall of Fame. Many of those Old Testament winners were poor in this life, but very rich in the life to come. I like what was said of their fiber: "The world was not worthy of them." What an honor!

No Mercedes could match that.

29 Envy

Color Me Green

Let us not become conceited, provoking and envying each other (Gal. 5:26).

Heliogabalus was a Roman emperor and a very envious man. And what could an already-wealthy man like that want? Power. Heliogabalus was envious of the powerful Senate. So he invited them to a spectacular Roman feast. While the senators guzzled down the wine, old Helio was playing it cool. As soon as the guests were drunker 'n Hootie Brown, he left the hall. He locked the doors and watched as the big bash went on.

Finally the emperor went up to the next floor and shouted down to the senators through a glass door in the ceiling. He told them that since they were always ambitious for fresh laurels, they should like his next surprise. Suddenly wreaths and flowers began to fall on them. Like a rainstorm the flowers fell, until the statesmen cried, "Enough, enough!" But the flower blizzard continued. Fearing for their lives, the men ran to the doors, but they were locked. They could not escape. When the last flower had fallen, every senator had suffocated, and Heliogabalus had satisfied his envy.

Where does envy come from? What provokes it? Why do we feel discontent when we drive by a beautiful mansion? Or when we see a sleek sports car? Or when we hear that So-and-so is taking our dream vacation to the Swiss Alps? Or when we learn that the neighbor down the street has just won first place in the *Reader's Digest* Sweepstakes?

Comparisons. That's the root beneath envy. It is looking at somebody else's possessions, achievements, good luck, or whatever, then staring back in disappointment at our own. Envy is the ugly emotion of being upset with "less." As long as we wish to make comparisons with other people, we'll be able to find somebody who has more.

Paul had some words for people who play comparison games. He said, ". . . When they measure themselves by themselves and compare themselves with themselves, they are not wise" (2 Cor. 10:12). The reason is that we usually end up salivating over somebody else's junk. Convulsions set in, and we turn a dark shade of green. (Remember the green-eyed dragon?)

Green. That reminds me of a myth—the one about greener grass. Who started that rumor, anyway? Whose big idea was it to say that "the grass is always greener on the other side of the fence"? His words must have been sarcastic. Because it's more like another fellow put it: "If the grass is greener on the other side of the fence, you can bet his water bill is higher."

The myth of the greener grass reminds me of a cartoon I once saw. In it there were several pastures divided by barbed-wire fences. Starting at the left and moving to the right, the fields got greener. Each field had a mule. The mules were sticking their heads through the fences, eating the "greener" grass. A few of them were all tangled up in the barbed wire, and none of them was interested in his own spacious field. And what about the one with the "greenest" grass? He was sitting on his rump with a hoof propping up his head, a look of boredom on his face. The cartoonist had written a one-word caption: "DISCONTENT."

Scripture records many accounts of envious people, but two of the worst illustrate how it can get out of hand.

The brother's keeper. Cain? Good guess, if you remember how Cain's offering of "fruits of the soil" was rejected by God, while Abel's sacrificing some of his flock was looked upon with favor. I'll bet I know a question you've always wondered about: Why didn't God accept Cain's offering? I mean—Wow!—he liked Abel's offering. Wasn't that sort of being cruel to Cain? I used to wonder the same thing.

The key idea to grab is that Abel's offering was an *animal* sacrifice. In the Old Testament an animal's shed blood was symbolic of what Jesus would do by dying as the Lamb of God. Knowing that, Cain still brought vegetables instead.

To encourage him, God gave him a special-delivery reminder: "Then the Lord said to Cain, 'Why are you angry? Why is your face downcast? *If you do what is right, will you not be accepted?*' " (Gen. 4:6–7a, italics added).

In other words, Cain knew what was right, but he just didn't want to do it. Envy was eating him up. The next day he did his dastardly deed: "Now Cain said to his brother Abel, 'Let's go out to the field.' And while they were in the field, Cain attacked his brother Abel and killed him" (v. 8).

Then he smarted off to God, "Am I my brother's keeper?" The answer to that is "Yes!" But Cain, because of envy, had become his brother's *killer*.

Instant replay. Why did the chief priests want Jesus dead? Because he revealed that their sacrifices were worthless. His life was an indictment against their fakery.

> "Do you want me to release to you the king of the Jews?" asked Pilate, knowing it was out of envy that the chief priests had handed Jesus over to him. But the chief priests stirred up the crowd to have Pilate release Barabbas instead (Mark 15:9–11).

When God gave them a second chance to accept Jesus—the correct offering—in envy, they infuriated the mob. They took "vegetables" (Barabbas) instead. Envy will break every commandment to get its way.

Envying is a lousy way to spend your life. How sad to be duped by the myth of the greener grass! All about us are brothers and sisters who need us to *keep* them, not *take* them. No voice screams louder in the face of the Contentment Commandment than that of envy.

What better proof is there than Heliogabalus?

30 Security

In His Shadow

And my God will meet all your needs according to his glorious riches in Christ Jesus (Phil. 4:19).

In John Bunyan's famous allegory, *The Pilgrim's Progress,* the incident is told of how Christian decides to leave the Main Highway and travel on another Path that looks easier. It turns out to be a big mistake; it leads him into the territory of Giant Despair, who owns Doubting Castle.

As you might guess, Christian gets captured by Giant Despair and thrown in a dungeon. He is advised to commit suicide. The giant discourages him from wasting his time with a stupid journey. When it appears that Christian is about to cash in his chips, Hope, Christian's traveling buddy, reminds him of previous victories. So he holds on to Hope and begins to pray.

Dawn is the inspiration Christian needs. As if a ray of sunshine has just struck his soul, he exclaims, "What a fool am I thus to lie in a stinking dungeon, when I may as well be at liberty. I have a Key in my bosom called Promise that will, I am persuaded, open any lock in Doubting Castle." Hope calls back, "That's good news. Good Brother, pluck it out of thy bosom and try." Immediately the prison gates fly wide open!

Beautiful insight: God's promises are the key to our contentment. We do not need new gods to keep us secure . . . or traditional spiritual rituals . . . or macho swear words that boost our ego . . . or Sabbath days . . . or freedom from authority, especially parental . . . or displays of violence to prove our "bravery" . . . or bought sex to make us feel important . . . or big piles of greenbacks . . . or the AWOL syndrome . . . or a red Mercedes with a black interior. In other words, the substance behind the Ten Commandments lies in God's promises. We can count on God to keep us secure and content, because he says he will. Never can you know the comfort of real security until you rest in the Lord.

God provides. I love to cheer myself with the Bible stories of God's miraculous provisions. It's hard to pick a favorite. But "The Birdman of Kerith Ravine" ranks in the top five. Who? Oh, sorry, you know him better as Elijah. The story is too good to paraphrase:

> Then the word of the LORD came to Elijah: "Leave here, turn eastward and hide in the Kerith Ravine, east of the Jordan. You will drink from the brook, and I have ordered the ravens to feed you there."
> So he did what the LORD had told him. He went to the Kerith Ravine, east of the Jordan, and stayed there. The ravens brought him bread and meat in the morning and bread and meat in the evening, and he drank from the brook (1 Kings 17:2–6).

Three things made this a miracle:

1. There was a drought and famine in the land.
2. God named the place and made it happen there.
3. Ravens are meat-eating scavenger birds, but they didn't gobble down Elijah's supper.

Shame on us for not resting secure in God's promise to provide our needs. As Poe put it, "Quoth the Raven, 'Nevermore!'"

God protects. Remember who took the Birdman's place? Elisha. One time he got a king mad at him. Bad move. The king sent several squads of soldiers down to a town called Dothan to fetch him for a head-chopping ceremony—his own! When Elisha's servant saw the army surrounding the city, he went into a frenzy. But we read: "'Don't be afraid,' the prophet answered. 'Those who are with us are more than those who are with them'" (2 Kings 6:16).

I can just see the servant scratching his head and cocking one eyebrow higher than the other, as if to say, "You've lost your mind, old boy. There are two of us. Have you been turning water into wine?"

Elisha's security is shown by what he did next:

> And Elisha prayed, "O LORD, open his eyes so he may see." Then the LORD opened the servant's eyes, and *he looked and saw the hills full of horses and chariots of fire all around Elisha* (2 Kings 6:17, italics added).

I'll bet he wrote home to Mom about that!

Never is there cause to covet some *thing* to give us security when we already have *Someone*! It's just a matter of pulling out of your pocket the Key called Promise and sticking it in the lock of Doubting Castle.

We've been at this for quite a while. That is, taking apart these commandments and putting them back together again. What do you say we rephrase the Ten Biggies into easy-to-grasp terms. Okay?

1. Don't be disloyal by playing with plastic gods.
2. Knock off with the religious trinkets. God is the only Real Thing.
3. Watch your heart, before your mouth gets out of order.
4. Try to match your rest day with your worship day instead of playing golf and going water-skiing.
5. Never get too smart, too busy, or too old to love your parents. Keep the family ties strong.
6. Keep a cool head, not a cold heart.
7. Let every man drool over his own wife; and let every wife drool over her own husband.
8. Don't put your fingers into someone else's cookie jar unless you're giving them some cookies.

9. Be a window. Lighten up, before you go over the wall and commit the ultimate fib.
10. Want only your own stuff. God will take care of you.

One last thing: funnel everything about these Ten Commandments through "The Chapter Before Chapter One." In fact, why not read that introduction again before you go out to conquer the world? Grace to you!

Step into a challenging world—and live a challenging life!